"Everything seems to be ready ...is everybody ready?"

"...is every

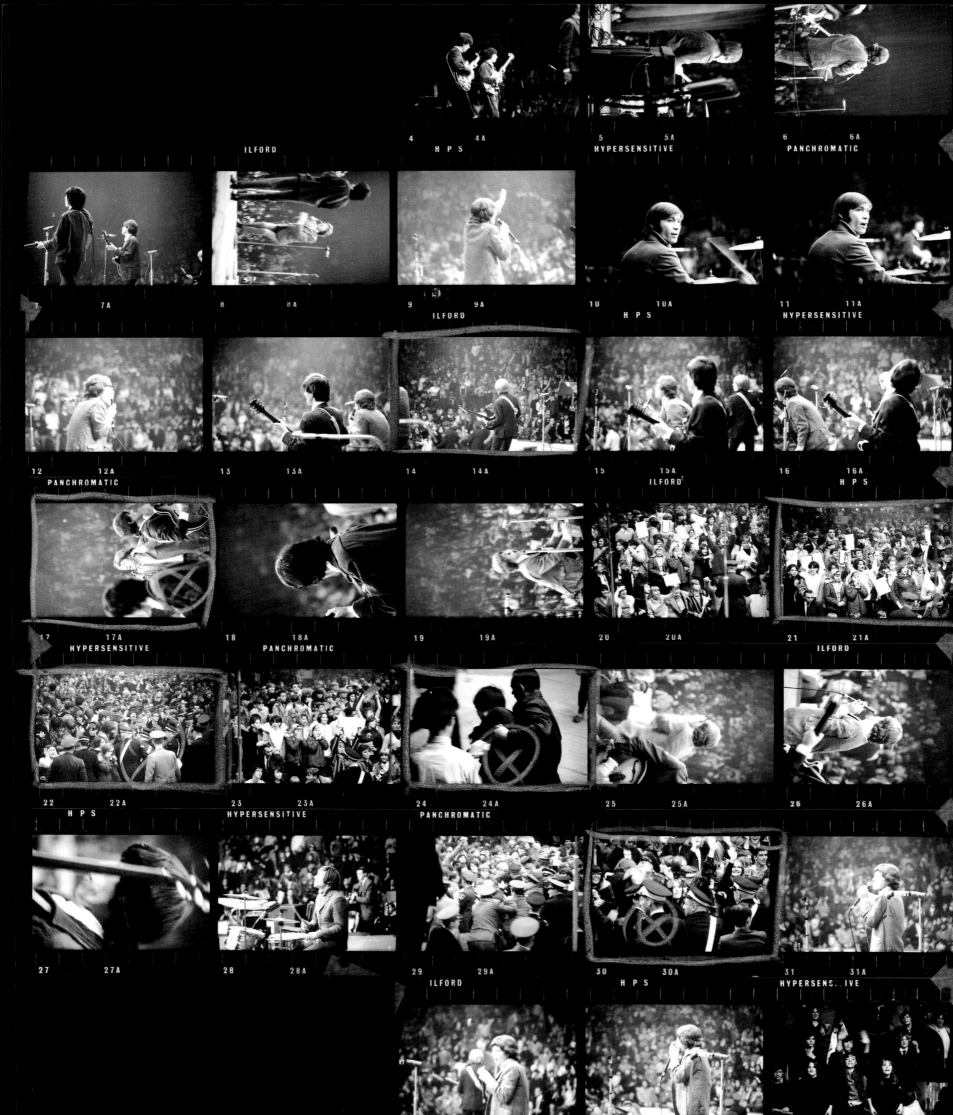

THE ROLLING STONES

A LIFE ON THE ROAD

INTERVIEWS BY JOOLS HOLLAND AND DORA LOEWENSTEIN

PENGUIN
STUDIO

FOREWORD

BY JOOLS HOLLAND

For the uninitiated the Rolling Stones are without question the greatest rock'n'roll group in the world. They are the most successful touring group on earth, covering more cities and people than any other live act. This book is the story of their touring. From the days when they argued about who sat in the front of a battered van while gigging round London public houses in the early 1960s to the time when they had to debate whether it was right to swop their private 747 jumbo jet for a reduced wheelbased 737, all because the runways of smaller airports - like Boston - couldn't take the weight of a jumbo when they were arriving with their huge entourage to play the local Enormodome.

No matter whether they are playing small pubs or a huge stadium, they always pull out all the stops and perform a show that comes from the heart. That, perhaps, is the only thing a book cannot totally communicate: the physical excitement that the group consistently generates on stage. I strongly recommend that once you have read this book, to fully appreciate the subject matter, take it along to one of the live shows and stand on it, where it will help to give you an improved view.

When I was growing up and learning about music I listened to blues and rhythm and blues records. I loved the recordings and the performers, but sometimes it was hard to identify with them because their lifestyles and culture were so distant from my own. Then I discovered the Rolling Stones playing music that had the same effect on me. But there were some very important differences. Although strongly influenced by the blues, they were not copyists: they had invented a whole new style of their own and, like me, they were alive and from London.

It was unrealistic for me to aspire to be an Albert Ammons or Little Richard, because I was from a different time and place, but I could be like a Rolling Stone. And their influence on me has come out in the recordings I have made with Squeeze and my own orchestra. The Rolling Stones managed to achieve something that is very difficult. They create music that is beautiful, exciting, lazy and rude, all at the same time.

It was therefore a privilege and a learning experience to interview them for this book. I discovered, through my routine enquiries, that they were artists, humorists, historians, hard men and gentlemen. When these natural musicians play together there is always a magical spark. I am grateful, because I have learnt from them much about an approach to music and life. If they decide to break the group up I would like to invite them to be my personal gurus.

FOREWORD

BY DORA LOEWENSTEIN

My experience of Life On The Road with the Rolling Stones began relatively recently and I wished to create something lasting which would reflect the unique quality and excellence of this magical band's live performances.

Thirty-odd years is no small period of time. It seems alien to all of us that in the early 60s when rock'n'roll was entering into people's homes for the first time that the Establishment looked upon the Rolling Stones and their contemporaries as loutish hooligans that were upsetting the very essence and order of life as they knew it. Now, in stark contrast, the Rolling Stones are welcomed into embassies around the world and doors are open to them wherever they go.

In the creation of this book the Rolling Stones were particularly keen to show the changes they have witnessed over the years and together we have tried to highlight the great contrasts between performing then and now.

In 1963 there was no music industry, no mass media, it was hard to travel the globe. In 1963 a sole VW combi van transported the Rolling Stones around the UK to perform in pubs and concert halls. In 1998 the music industry is global, mass media has transformed into 'multi-media', and any corner of the world can be accessed within a day. These days the Rolling Stones travel the road with over 300 permanent employees, and have been known to have three 747 aeroplanes transporting them and their equipment from one side of the world to the other. The difference speaks for itself.

Working on this book has been a very rewarding and interesting experience for me. To know a group of people well and to observe what they do from afar is completely different from working with them. At first it is easy to assume that when a group of musicians as well established as the Stones embark on a tour of the world that their work begins and ends with their stage performance. Scratch the surface just a bit and you find one of the largest, most complex travelling productions equal only to large military operations. As for the Stones themselves, their days are filled with a plethora of activities which swallow any spare time they may wish to have: new videos to shoot, alterations to their set, press interviews, sound checks, local dignitaries to entertain, and then it's on to the next place.

This book is about the touring life of the Stones, but I hope it gives the genuine feel of life on the road as it is a work that has in essence been born out of the road. The Stones and I first started talking about this project in Washington at the beginning of their Voodoo Lounge tour in August 1994. Since then, after many visits to them around the globe both on Voodoo Lounge and Bridges To Babylon, we began to see the book take shape.

I wish this book to give all its readers an opportunity to get a glimpse of how these years of travelling have been and the many remarkable moments of entertainment that this most famous and exceptional band has brought to the world. Also I hope that it evokes the feeling of constant movement and evolution that life on the road demands. Finally I would like this book to be a tribute to the Rolling Stones, and to what they do best.

MICK: I used to like marching bands. The military bands of different regiments that I heard on the radio when I was a small child. But I never went to any music or dance or plays: THE PANTOMIME WAS THE ONLY LARGE SHOW I WAS EVER TAKEN TO. I LOVED IT.

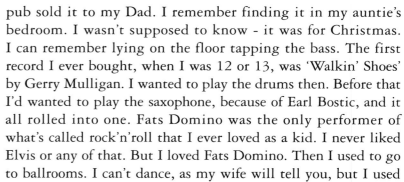

KEITH: GUS DUPREE, MY GRANDFATHER, TURNED ME ON TO THE GUITAR BY NOT ALLOWING ME TO PLAY IT. THAT WAS A FUCKING BRILLIANT TRICK. He played violin, saxophone and guitar. He'd had to give up the sax because he got gassed in the First World War and that blew his lungs. So he took up violin. When I used to visit him off the Seven Sisters Road there was an upright piano, and on top was this guitar, but I couldn't reach it. In any

case, you couldn't touch it. You wouldn't even dream of it - "that's Grandad's". But what I found out years after he died was that he only put it up there when he knew I was coming. So the son of a bitch had me spotted from when I was this high. Then when I was about ten or eleven I asked him if I could play the guitar, and he said "If you're going to play the guitar you've got to learn this one thing called 'Malagueña'. If you play that you can play the guitar." He led me in that way. We'd go out to take the dog for a walk and we'd be out for two days, and end up in Charing Cross Road, round the back in Ivor Mairants' guitar store. I knew all the guys who built and repaired guitars. They used to sit me up on a shelf, give me a cup of tea and biscuits, and the glue would be bubbling away. I got introduced to music like that: I'd see broken violins going by and watch the guys fixing them with that smell of glue. I only knew the back way in. It's been the story of my life ever since - always round the tradesman's entrance.

CHARLIE: I got my first drum kit when I was thirteen or fourteen. It was an Olympic: a guy in a

pub sold it to my Dad. I remember finding it in my auntie's bedroom. I wasn't supposed to know - it was for Christmas. I can remember lying on the floor tapping the bass. The first record I ever bought, when I was 12 or 13, was 'Walkin' Shoes' by Gerry Mulligan. I wanted to play the drums then. Before that I'd wanted to play the saxophone, because of Earl Bostic, and it all rolled into one. Fats Domino was the only performer of what's called rock'n'roll that I ever loved as a kid. I never liked Elvis or any of that. But I loved Fats Domino. Then I used to go to ballrooms. I can't dance, as my wife will tell you, but I used to watch the drummer. My first real impression of drummers would be Phil Seamen, Chico Hamilton, those kind of players. I remember seeing Georgie Fame playing at the Allnighter with a guy called Red Rees - he was the first really good soul-type drummer, I suppose.

BILL: Towards the end of the war, when I was about five or six, my brothers and sisters used to play a little wind-up record player in my Gran's house down the road in Sydenham - the Andrews Sisters and Glenn Miller, Frank Sinatra when he started. And they used to swoon over all these singers. I find a lot of songs that I listened to then give me a really nice, sad nostalgia. Before I took up an instrument I heard something that really did astound me: Les Paul and Mary Ford singing 'The World Is Waiting For The Sunrise'. I heard the electric guitar and that amazing stuff Les Paul did: I've been a fan ever since. I always wanted to be in a band, because I'd done some piano lessons as a really small boy, passed two grades. But then I wanted to play football and cricket and wouldn't practise.

RON: My brothers Art and Ted had a music room at the back of the house with a little hatch through from the kitchen. They had a skiffle group - Lawrence Sheaf was one of the guys, a great guitar player who played like Big Bill Broonzy, and I used to sit there and think 'That looks like a good job'. Art knew a few chords, and the banjo player Jim Willis taught me - he used to write little dots on the strings - finger one, two, three. I just tried to go from there, playing along to Chris Barber records and some American imports of Chuck Berry which I used to know note for note. And I went in a van with my brothers and various members of their band to Finsbury Park to see Duke Ellington. I was still in short pants. THE FIRST ALBUM I EVER BOUGHT WAS A COUNT BASIE. AND THE FIRST TWO SINGLES WERE 'GREAT BALLS OF FIRE' AND 'I'M WALKIN''. That was a good start, wasn't it?

MICK: I used to do concerts with different bands in sitting rooms, around Dartford, Bexley Heath. Jerry Lee Lewis, Buddy Holly, that sort of thing. Most of it was just rehearsing - we didn't really do that many live shows.

CHARLIE: I used to play with a bass player called David Green who lived next door: we used to go and play in pubs with the local jazz mainstream.

We played skiffle as well, and the first proper gig was at Wimbledon Palais in some terrible skiffle band. We used to have these awful jerseys with the singer's initials on. We looked a bit like Frankie Lymon and the Teenagers except that our jerseys were horrible, they'd been washed too many times.

KEITH: I really learnt how to play the guitar at art school; it was full of guitar players. In the late 50s and early 60s very little art got done but a lot of guitar playing went down. My first gig had been with a guy called Mike Ross at Sidcup Art School. Of course we didn't get paid for it. It was some little school and we played country songs, just him and me. It must have been bloody awful. All I know is that we spent the night in the bus shelter by a park. There was one bitch who was very nice to us but didn't put out. I was about 14 or 15, and this was my first gig, missing the last train, stuck in a bus shelter with one slag and the other guitar player. That was my introduction to show business. And the next time I played in public was with the Stones.

BILL: The only way you could be in a band in those days was to be a very high quality player because there were only dance bands, so I never saw the possibility. I did clarinet for a couple of years at school but I didn't like that. Then when skiffle came in I was in the RAF in Northern Germany: we heard skiffle coming through on British Forces Network, but we tuned into the American Forces Network and I heard my first rock'n'roll in 1955. Suddenly I was listening to Elvis, Little Richard, Fats Domino, Jerry Lee, Chuck Berry, and that's when I really wanted to do it. I was in Germany listening to that stuff probably half a year before they hit England. I was coming home with records of Little Richard when they hadn't really heard of him, so I was a little bit ahead of all that. The film Rock Rock Rock came out and everybody kind of laughed at Chuck Berry, they thought he was a comedy act, doing 'You Can't Catch Me', with the duck walk - everybody laughed in the cinema and I was awestruck.

RON: My first band was called the Thunderbirds. We were doing things like 'It Takes A Worried Man' and 'Down By The Riverside', skiffle - a tea-case bass, banjo... and I was on washboard. The first gig I did with a famous person was at the Ivy League Club in West Drayton by Heathrow, where my Mum still lives. Memphis Slim. My group had to back him up and we got a bottle of whiskey as payment. The Thunderbirds dropped the Thunder because of Chris Farlowe's band. And then

we got into trouble for nicking the American Byrds' name. Our manager at the time took it upon himself, without telling us, to sue them as soon as they landed on English soil. I was speaking to Jim McGuinn about this. I said "Do you remember, when you first came to England, getting served with a writ as you got off the plane?" He said "Yes I do, it really spoilt our arrival". We made the front page of the Melody Maker - BIRDS SUE BYRDS - it was so

embarrassing. And there was this long silence with Jim McGuinn and he went "You bastard". And then he gave me a hug.

BILL: We put this band together called the Cliftons, just four or five local people, and that was my first gig, a little dance hall in Penge, the Starlight Ballroom. We were just a five piece, a drummer, three guitars and a singer and we all plugged into one little Watkins Westminster amp, with four inputs and an echo chamber. There wasn't room for me so I took a Grundig tape recorder, plugged my guitar into the Record socket and it came out of the speakers. That's how amateur it was. The Cliftons were playing the popular R&B stuff, Lloyd Price's 'Stack-O-Lee', Chuck Berry, Fats Domino. The Little Richard we could sort of manage with someone singing a bit like that, but it was pretty hard. We got quite serious and did well in South London, out into Essex, Croydon, but we used to work for villains, so you'd end up never getting paid. Then it started to fall apart a bit.

OUR DRUMMER WENT AND ANSWERED AN AD FOR A DRUMMER WITH A BLUES BAND IN CHELSEA CALLED THE ROLLING STONES.

CHARLIE: ALEXIS KORNER ASKED ME TO JOIN HIS BAND, AND AT THE FIRST REHEARSAL I MET A FRIEND WHO PLAYED THE BASS, AND I MET MY WIFE. The first nine months I was in Alexis's band and when I left I played in a band with Geoff Bradford. They were wonderful players. I met Brian through Alexis and Mick sang with us a couple of times. Ronnie Jones used to sing, but he couldn't get time away from the army or the air force, wherever he was, and we'd need a singer so Mick did those bits.

BILL: I built this bass out of something we managed to buy for next to nothing, this horrible thing. I put it on a fretwork machine, reshaped it, took all the strings off, put a new pick-up in, polished it and made it into this magical, miniature thing, which I've still got and used with the Stones way into the 1980s. Ian Stewart used to call it 'the Flying Penge'.

MICK: Eventually I was playing the blues with Keith, Dick Taylor who was eventually in the Pretty Things, and some other people. Then we met Brian and Charlie through Alexis Korner at the Ealing Club. We'd seen this advertisement and we said "Oh, this sounds like it might be interesting, a blues band. We're a blues band, we should go and see this". We'd never heard of Alexis Korner, thought he was in the trad scene, and we weren't really into that. I hated all that to be honest. But then we went up to the Ealing Club and met Brian, Charlie, Ben, and Stu at some point. Alexis was a great introducer, and everyone sort of knew everyone else. Half the audience were musicians - people like John Baldry, Paul Jones, Cyril Davies the harmonica player and a guitar player who was quite good called Geoff Bradford. It was like a showcase. Geoff Bradford would get up and play two numbers, Brian would get up and play like Elmore James for a couple of numbers, I would get up and do some Chuck Berry or Jimmy Reed, and Keith would play. Alexis moved onto the Marquee, which was kind of a big deal, so we decided that we would form a band with some of these people. We still didn't have a drummer and we'd pick up drummers and so on, which was very unsatisfactory.

KEITH: The first rehearsal of what turned out to be the Stones was at the Bricklayers Arms in Soho. I went upstairs and there was Ian Stewart sitting playing boogie woogie and keeping an eye on his bike which was chained to a parking meter. All the time the strippers are walking by, with their bouffant hair, wigs and little pink bags, going from one club to another, and Stu's still playing. He took no notice of me as I walked in either.

MICK: We used to rehearse in Soho upstairs at the Bricklayers Arms pub. Hours and days we'd rehearse. We played a lot of rehearsals and no gigs.

KEITH: It seemed like we rehearsed for ages. We didn't do a gig for months. We had a great boogie woogie piano player and a couple of interesting fledgling guitar players and an enthusiastic singer and harp player. And that was it. You do need a rhythm section, and that was the one thing we were lacking and couldn't afford.

BILL: The drummer in the Cliftons went up and played with the Stones on a couple of dates when we weren't playing. He came back with a reel-to-reel copy of some Jimmy Reed stuff and said "There ain't no bass player. He's left and if you want to have a gig, they're looking for a bass player." I was married and had a little kid, nine months old. Times were really hard, we were living in poverty. I said "I don't know, I'm not sure" but I listened to this Jimmy Reed stuff and I thought 'Well, that's really something else, that's way out there, not commercial'. We loaded all the equipment up and went to the Wetherby Arms at World's End in Chelsea. I met them for the first time and thought they were a load of beatniks. Coming from South East London I had more of a teddy boy image, those kind of clothes and attitude, and trying to keep a job together, being a bit normal. I brought all the gear in and they were really over the top about it. They weren't sure about me because I was playing a more rock'n'roll sort of style than they were used to. I'd been doing gigs with Richie Valens, the lower echelon of those pop singers of the late 50s and early 60s, so I'd got quite a good grasp of a lot of styles. The Stones said "What do you play?" I said "Well, a bit of rock'n'roll and sort of R&B". I said "Fats Domino", and they didn't like that, and "Jerry Lee Lewis" and they went "Uurgh" and "Chuck Berry" and they said "Oh, good, yeah".

KEITH: One day we picked up a drummer called Tony Chapman who was our first regular drummer. Terrible. One of the worst... Cat would start a number and end up either four times as fast as he started it or three times as slow. We did say, "Hey, Tony, d'y'know any bass players?" He said "I do know one". "Tell him to come to the next rehearsal". So we all turned up and in walks... Bill Wyman, ladies and gentlemen. Huge speaker he's got, and a spare Vox A30 amp which is the biggest amp we've ever seen in our lives.

BILL: I GOT A BIG SPEAKER CABINET MADE WITH A GOODMANS 18-INCH SPEAKER AND SOME CONCRETE IN THE BOTTOM, AND ONE OF THOSE BUILD-IT-YOURSELF 25 WATT AMPLIFIERS. EVERY TIME YOU TOUCHED IT YOU GOT ELECTROCUTED - YOU KNEW YOU WERE GOING TO GET ELECTROCUTED BUT YOU HAD TO PLUG IN. IT WAS A TERRIBLE THING. NO ONE WOULD GO NEAR IT.

CHARLIE: We rehearsed in the pub on the corner. I remember going inside and Bill Wyman had this big green amp. That's all we had him in the band for, rumour has it.

BILL: They had fuck all gear. Two terrible little amplifiers that were totally ruined: the speakers were all smashed, but it sounded good for the music. But they really liked my gear, and when I brought the huge speaker in, my wardrobe, they were a bit enamoured with that. We seemed to hit it off pretty quickly in fact, but the drummer wasn't very good, he'd speed up and slow down. Ian Stewart I'd met before in his neck of the woods in Sutton,

I knew him vaguely. Mick was very friendly and chatty. Brian and Keith just acted like I wasn't there, actually. Which they do do, or they did do later. It was their normal behaviour. I thought they were fucking rude, and thought 'If they don't want to talk to me, I don't want to talk to them'. They didn't want to know about me until I got my fag packet out and bought a couple of drinks and then they were a bit more chatty.

KEITH: WE JUST WANTED A GIG, WE DIDN'T GIVE A SHIT, MONEY OR NOT. THE ONLY REASON MONEY CAME INTO IT WAS BECAUSE TO GET CHARLIE WATTS WE HAD TO BE ABLE TO OFFER HIM A CERTAIN AMOUNT. The desire to get Charlie was one of the driving forces that nailed this band together, because we knew he had to be the drummer. If you didn't spring for a can for the drum kit you've got to be able to offer the guy at least as much if not more than he'd get somewhere else. It's a matter of sheer economics. It was a conspiracy on our part, I realise in retrospect - we've got to keep going long enough to offer Charlie a certain amount, hey £5.00 a week, or three solid gigs to get him. There was a certain break-even point. It was all to get him, that was the only reason we struggled on. And when Alexis Korner gave up Charlie for Ginger Baker we rubbed our hands with glee: he's coming our way. We actually stole him off Ronnie's older brother's band, that was the night we stole him.

CHARLIE: I was in about four bands. I used to play with Art Wood - Ronnie's brother - and a great tenor player, Art Themen. So the Stones were just another band.

MICK: First of all there weren't that many good drummers in England, period. There was Phil Seamen, Ginger Baker, some jazz drummers. But no one really understood this music which was all these shuffles or straight eights. We played with Carlo Little and the bass player from Screaming Lord Sutch's bands, but we couldn't get them permanently because they were sought after and we had hardly any shows. And we auditioned the drummer of the Kinks, Mick Avory - very unsatisfactory for us, but he turned out all right for the Kinks. Once we got together with Charlie it seemed to work very well.

BILL: They asked Charlie to join and they fired my drummer. It was difficult for me because he had a temper on him and went bright red and said "Come on Bill, let's go and form a new band" and I had to make a decision at that second - I didn't know about Charlie - and I said "No, I think I'll stay for a while, I like this". So he stormed off in a huff because we were kind of mates, and I stayed and Charlie joined. And the moment Charlie joined I could suddenly play much better because he was so good to play with.

KEITH: 'Love Me Do' came out and it was a sudden attack from the North. Jesus Christ. We thought we were the only guys in the world, which stretched to Watford as far as we were concerned. We're playing Muddy Waters and Jimmy Reed. We ain't got a gig yet, but we know we're the hottest shit in town, and you've always got to believe that, especially at the beginning.

CHARLIE: Mick rented a flat in Edith Grove; I've got a feeling nobody else helped with the rent. It was more convenient for me to live there than go all the way home to Wembley. That's where I learnt about Jimmy Reed and all that because Brian would play it all day on his bloody great gramophone thing. I learnt R&B in that period, living and playing it constantly. The Stones are very lucky in many ways, but they certainly were in that Brian was a fanatic. He'd ring up the Melody Maker and complain that there was no real R&B played in London and then send letters. So he got a foot in the doorway in the Marquee Club and the 100 Club and once we'd played there people liked it and we got more and more work. It wasn't necessarily me, but when I joined we would have one gig in three weeks, then we'd have four, then six and in the end I was on the road all the time.

KEITH: BRIAN CAME UP WITH THE NAME. IT WAS A PHONE CALL - WHICH COST MONEY - AND WE WERE DOWN TO PENNIES. WE'D GOT NO GAS AND WE WERE FREEZING OUR BALLS OFF, NO WATER, EVERYTHING WAS CUT OFF. WE GOT A GIG AT LAST, SO WE SAID "CALL UP JAZZ NEWS, PUT IN AN ADVERT". SO BRIAN GAILY DIALS AWAY - AND THEY SAY "WHO?"! WE HADN'T GOT A NAME AND EVERY SECOND WAS COSTING A PRECIOUS FARTHING. THERE'S A MUDDY WATERS RECORD FACE DOWN - THE BEST OF MUDDY WATERS - AND THE FIRST SONG WAS 'ROLLIN' STONE BLUES'. BRIAN HAD A PANICKED LOOK ON HIS FACE - HE SAID "I DON'T KNOW... THE ROLLIN' STONES". THAT'S THE REASON WE'RE CALLED THE ROLLING STONES, BECAUSE IF HE DIDN'T OPEN HIS MOUTH IMMEDIATELY WE WERE GOING TO STRANGLE HIM AND CUT HIM OFF. NOT A LOT OF THOUGHT WENT INTO IT, IN OTHER WORDS.

MICK: The name was from the Muddy Waters song. I think I came up with it but I don't remember really. We advertised for gigs - I don't think we got anything from the ad. We got one or two gigs around: Stu would try and get us gigs in these suburban places like his local, the Red Lion in Sutton.

CHARLIE: WHEN I STARTED IT WAS GOING TO BE A THREE MONTH THING, THEN A THREE YEAR THING. I ALWAYS SAID "IT WON'T LAST".

KEITH: **Our first gig was in the intervals at either the Ealing Club or the Marquee.**

Alexis Korner's band would take fifteen minutes to get boozed up again. There were a lot of people going for that slot, so you'd do it for nothing, just get up there. Alexis was a great encourager and Cyril Davies too, in his hard-nosed begrudging way - he never gave you any illusions, he was a panel-beater from Wembley, cauliflower ear, bent nose, played harp like a fucking little water rat. Cyril could say "fucking cunt" and that was a compliment.

It built up slowly over the 1962 period. The weekends suddenly got busy. We'd play Ken Colyer's 51 Club in the afternoon on the Charing Cross Road and then do a quick run out to Richmond for the whole night. That's where we cut our teeth. We were working in the same room every week, and we got to know it and hone down our shit, basically practise. They thought they were getting a show, and we were just rehearsing in public.

BILL: By the time Charlie joined we were doing three or four gigs a week. He joined in January 1963 and it just elevated from there. We were fighting the jazz promoters and agents who wanted to put the mockers on us. They used to give us gigs and at the last minute they'd cancel when you arrived, because they hated us, and trad jazz was starting to lose its appeal - they were trying to hang on in there.

MICK: It wasn't just old people who went to the trad jazz. We used to go to the Marquee on a trad night just to pick up girls. Mostly everyone was under 20.

KEITH: There was pop music and the alternative music of the day was traditional jazz, Dixieland, your Acker Bilks and Kenny Balls, a lot of good players but a bag thing - you didn't feel like there were any guys with lead pipes down their sharkskin suits. That was the area that put up a bit of a fight. When we started playing the intervals, they suddenly realised that they were getting nudged out of the way, and it was all happening in a matter of months, that quick. And suddenly we weren't getting interval slots because when the main band went on everybody had left, and the interval band had become the highspot. The jazz guys closed ranks. They must have felt threatened: it became quite vicious.

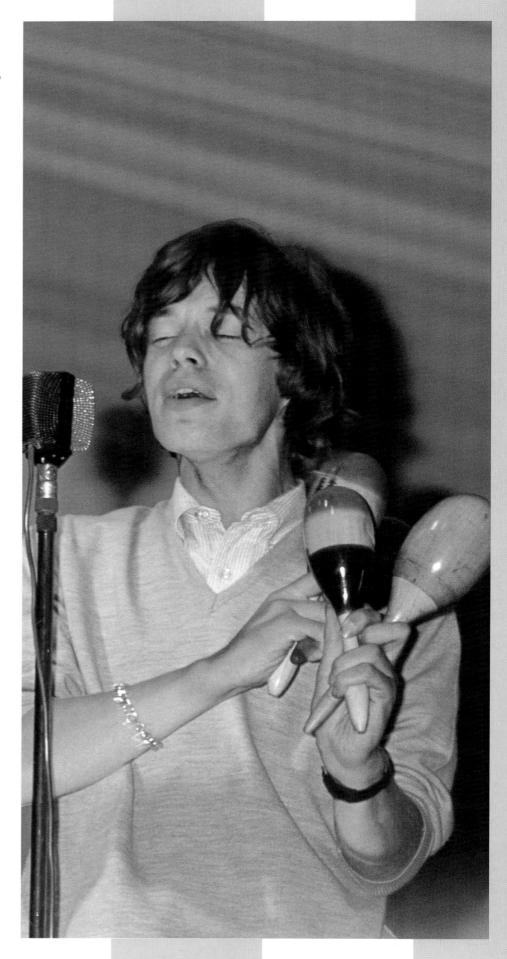

MICK: TRAD WAS ON A REAL DOWN. THEY DIDN'T LIKE US.

…But the promoters were pub owners and if the trad bands didn't bring in the punters, that was the end of that. Rock bands were taking over the trad clubs. They were called rhythm and blues bands because you couldn't call it a rock band if you were going to go into a traditional jazz club. It was a kind of musical snobbery, so we had to make a tremendous fuss about being a blues band and not a rock band, even though we played a lot of rock music by any definition.

BILL: When we were doing the Marquee interval for a blues night, a little night in the week, it suddenly became *the* big night - there were 800 people for us and only 300 to see Monty Sunshine the next day. So they kind of knocked us out of the Marquee, and all the other clubs were jazz clubs. The Ricky Tick started in Windsor, which was an R&B club for bands like us, but there weren't many places to play. Then Brian knew this Russian film-maker Giorgio Gomelsky who'd worked with the Chris Barber band and he had a bit of clout. He got us Eel Pie Island which we did once a week and we had a fantastic success there, doubled the audience right away. And he got us the Station Hotel in Richmond of course, which was the biggest one for us, because we got all the students coming in and that hit the newspapers.

CHARLIE: SOMETIMES WE PLAY CLUBS BEFORE THE START OF A TOUR AS A TRY-OUT.

IT'S A BIT LIKE HAVING A FERRARI:

WE SORT OF TAKE IT SLOWLY ROUND THE DRIVE
BEFORE GOING ON THE STRETCH.

KEITH: We decided to get some solid residency at the Crawdaddy Club, which was Richmond Station Hotel. We were trying to sound as close as we could to Muddy Waters, Jimmy Reed, Chuck Berry, depending on what song we were doing - Chicago blues, basically.

BILL: The Station Hotel took off in four weeks from nothing to about three or four hundred people - and the Beatles came to see us in April. We'd had Record Mirror there, the local press, and the Daily Mirror had written about us because of this madness going on. It was just insane: there'd be these huge queues on Sunday afternoon to get to see us and 400 people in the back of this pub. When we played it was the most magical thing you could imagine. I still can't really capture exactly what - just fantastic, the perfect club feel where you were in contact with everybody in this small room. The ceiling was really low and when we used to play those bloody Bo Diddley things, like 'Doing the Crawdaddy' and 'Pretty Thing' with that tremolo, we used to go on for twenty minutes on one track and the crowd were hypnotised, like a tribal thing. Everybody who just went for a cursory glance got sucked into it and said "God, you should hear what's going on down in Richmond".

KEITH **The Beatles kicked the doors open and we zoomed in behind them and held it open.**

MICK: The Beatles, the Cavern, all that was going on, but the media's in London. I think that the South of England was really interested in having their own little scene. Then suddenly they found out about this little blues scene, of which we were the most obvious kind of people.

KEITH: Most of our gigs were basically West London - Kingston, Richmond, Eel Pie Island. In town on Sundays at Ken Colyer's 51 Club, in Charing Cross Road, and there'd be these odd gigs in the East End, like Dalston: a great feeling, still some of the World War II spirit.

RON: Leo Clerk had a club in Windsor called the Cavern. I was queuing up outside the club, which was like a corrugated iron air raid shelter and this red Bedford van pulled up outside and the Stones piled out in orange tab-collared shirts, fell out the back. And then there was the equipment behind them and Stu unloading it for the gig. We were all waiting, while Alex Harvey was playing, and he went on and on. At the side you'd see Brian Jones come out with a bottle of beer, and a little glimpse of Mick waiting to go on, and meanwhile Alex Harvey's still doing 'Take Out Some Insurance On Me Baby'. The tension was mounting and when they finally got on it was really rocking.

BILL: The Beatles had been popular in England for a year, and were just about to go to America for the first time. They were doing Thank Your Lucky Stars at Shepperton or Teddington and just dropped in on their way back to London. We were playing and suddenly there they were, just standing there. Everyone else was just raving and here's these four silhouetted black leather overcoated people right in front of you. We had a chat in the interval and got really friendly with them - they stayed till the end and then we went back with them to the Chelsea flat in Edith Grove. They hung out all night with us, playing and talking about music.

BILL: **The Beatles really blew us away when they came down... We were all going "Fuck, that's the fucking Beatles, oh fuck".**

BILL: Andrew Loog Oldham came down with Eric Easton in April or May, after the Beatles had come. He was tipped off by a guy called Peter Jones of Record Mirror to go down to Richmond to see this band. Andrew had worked with the Beatles, but I don't know whether he'd checked with them. Andrew and Eric started chatting to us, asking us if we wanted to sign a management and recording deal with them. So Brian, who was the leader of the band, dealt with that. We signed with them and on 10th May we made our first record. We had to choose a song to do and we didn't have any commercial songs, so we just went through all the songs we had, about a hundred of them, and they were all uncommercial. We finally plumped for Chuck Berry's 'Come On' and a Muddy Waters song called 'I Want To Be Loved', which we did quite regularly. We went in for a three-hour session and we didn't like it at all; they put it out and it was in the charts for about four months.

MICK: The material we were playing was really mixed because we felt it had to be. We were playing to more pop audiences. We changed the material a lot, didn't play Jimmy Reed stuff much, although we could if we had the opportunity. We played Solomon Burke things, slow soul ballads. We had a big hit with Arthur Alexander's 'You Better Move On'. And we used to do really terrible cover versions of the songs the Liverpool bands had made famous like 'Money' and 'Poison Ivy', songs that we used to do really badly, but were really popular with the punters in the ballrooms who couldn't understand the blues. We probably used to play the odd blues at the beginning of the evening.

RON: I walked to the Richmond Jazz and Blues Festival in the rugby ground. I'll never forget seeing this marquee like an elephant with a big bum, and you could hear the Stones doing 'Bye Bye Johnny' or something. I walked in and I was right at the back.

I REMEMBER WATCHING THESE GUYS LEANING DOWN FROM THE STAGE AT THE END WITH ALL THESE CHICKS AND I'M GOING "I LOVE IT".

Walking out of the marquee I smashed my leg on this big iron tent peg. I thought 'You'd better straighten up for this if you're ever going to be with them. Keith's going to give you a lot worse than that'. And, sure enough, to this day he still does.

CHARLIE: Andrew certainly got Mick and Keith writing and he got the band an image together. He was very good at that, very bright and wonderful for us at that time.

KEITH: When we started there was great joy at getting a recording contract, but at the same time this sense of death, because nobody lasted more than two years in the early 60s. It didn't matter how big you were, unless you were Elvis, you were supposed to disappear at the height of your career.

RON: The first time I saw them on TV it was 'Come On' I think, and 'I Want To Be Loved', the B-side, which I got them to play at rehearsals - they didn't care. I started it up and they all joined in and then they said "How does the rest of it go?" I said "Well, I'm your man, I know this inside out".

MICK: Television was easy really. In those days there were only two channels, so everybody watched these channels. It was a complete talking point the next day: who was on it. And how many pop shows were there? Two.

KEITH: A lot of changes occurred. Our sights were raised. We already thought we were the fucking king and his cousins. Andrew and I recognised the connection to art school and how to sell things. We said "We've got to turn these people on their hands, they're not going to know what happened to them in the record business and either we win or we lose - it's heads or tails". The Beatles were out there and doing some shit, two records out and both had gone to Number One - this was a big deal. And Andrew said "If you want to make records you've got to go down that pop path, to get in there and be able to manoeuvre a bit", because in those days you made a record and you'd just see guys in brown coats walking around and pointing a microphone saying "Stand here and do this". So we said "We'll just do what the Beatles don't", it was like not wearing a uniform.

BILL: People knew about us all of a sudden, we were on television doing Thank Your Lucky Stars, a few radio things, Saturday clubs, but we'd never gone outside London. So Andrew and Eric started to get us gigs in ballrooms in places like Baldock, out near Cambridge. It was hilarious because we'd go to Peterborough and play in this Civic Hall or church hall for 500-600 people and all the girls had 50s hairstyles and you'd be playing blues and a bit of Chuck Berry thrown in to speed it up. They didn't know what to do to the music. They couldn't dance to our music so they just stood and stared. The promoter would come up and have rows with us on stage: "Do some popular songs". We didn't want to know about it - "Fuck off", you know. The crowd stood and watched and at the end they really applauded, or they didn't care one way or the other; they weren't offensive. But the promoters didn't like it.

When we were going out in the ballrooms in June of 63 we were getting thirty quid a night all in, that was it, you had to get there, pay for the petrol, pay for food. There was nothing in it. So we always drove home, whether it was from Southend or Bristol or wherever. And I was still working in Streatham for a diesel engineers so I was getting in at four in the morning after doing the gig and getting up at six to go to work. I did that right through to August 1963. I couldn't do it anymore. I just wasn't getting any sleep. My mate was helping me out, you know, "Here comes the boss, wake up". Stu was the same. We used to both crash out on my front room floor, get in at 4.30 or something, go into the living room so we didn't wake the baby and crash out on the floor or the sofa or the chairs. Charlie packed up work about June, then Ian and I eventually both gave it up in August or September.

KEITH: THE FIRST PROPER TOUR WAS LATE SUMMER OF 63: LITTLE RICHARD, BO DIDDLEY, THE EVERLY BROTHERS AND A FEW OTHER WEIRDO ACTS LIKE US THROWN IN FOR GOOD MEASURE. WHAT AN EDUCATION - LIKE GOING TO ROCK'N'ROLL UNIVERSITY - SIX WEEKS WORKING WITH THESE GUYS EVERY NIGHT. YOU WANT TO KNOW ANYTHING ABOUT ROCK'N'ROLL, YOU'VE GOT THE WHOLE SPECTRUM THERE. They're the best teachers in the world and at the same time we're getting bigger and bigger on this tour, opening the second half of the show and the kids were rocking, and that's pissing the Everly Brothers off because they're top of the bill.

KEITH: You can hit the **back row** via the cameramen. You give them a **nod** and a **wink** - the back row's got it.

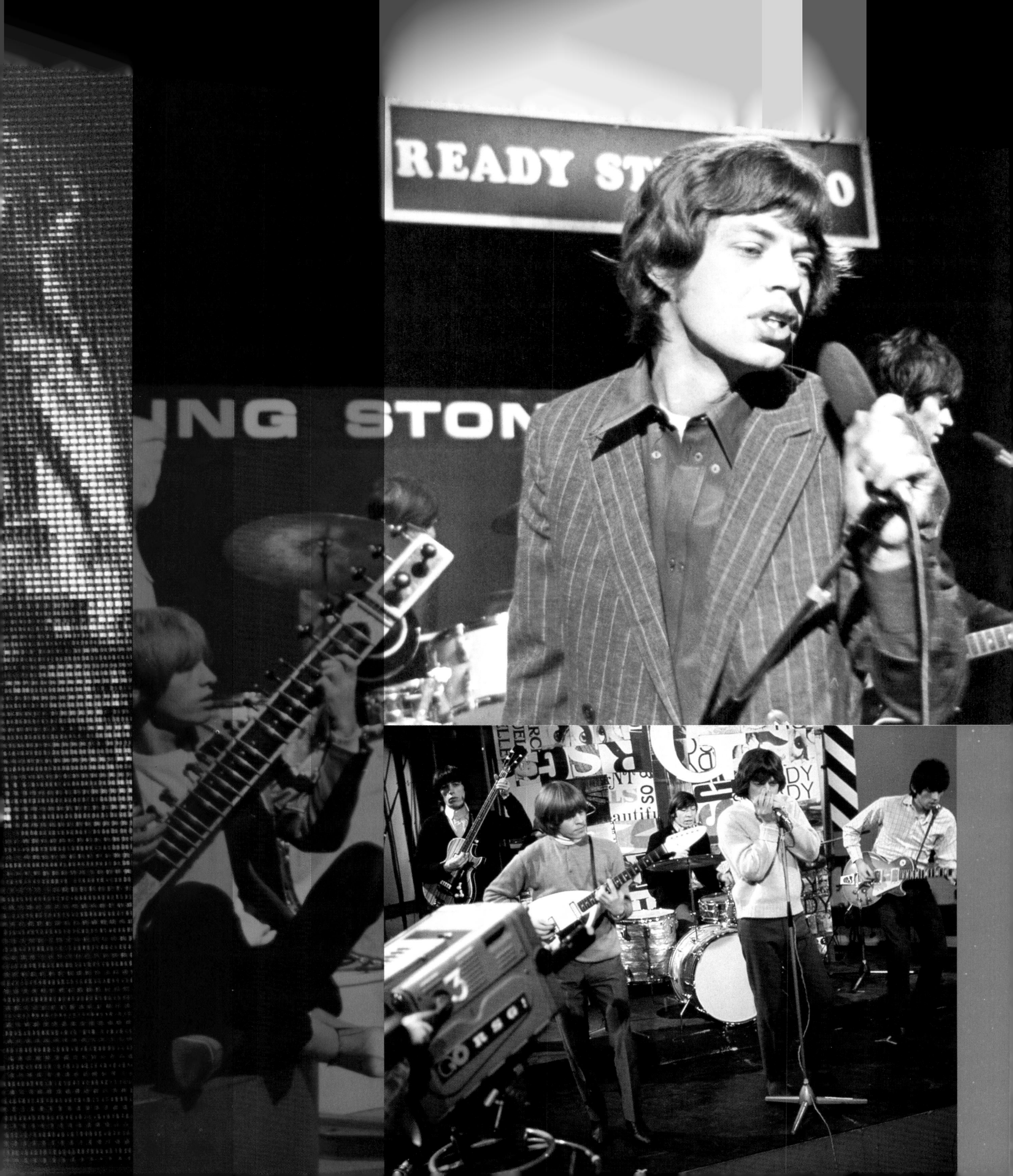
READY

MICK: The tour was totally different because that was another type of audience. A lot of people came to see the headliners like the Everly Brothers who'd never heard of the Rolling Stones. We were almost bottom of the bill and we only played two numbers, so we'd play our records, 'Come On', and one other, like 'Memphis, Tennessee', that they knew - and that was it. So we went from playing two hours at the Ealing Club to playing two numbers and it wasn't until the end of the 60s that we actually got back to playing the two hours again.

CHARLIE: We went into that world of playing twenty minutes and off, or three numbers. I liked it in a way because I'm lazy, but nothing happens, your hands get soft.

BILL: We were mad fans of Bo Diddley's, and great mates with him and Jerome Green the harmonica player, and the Everlys, so we always used to hang out and jam backstage in the dressing rooms. Little Richard was a bit funny. He looked like a banker. He was into his suit and all that by then, not any flamboyant gear. He'd already retired once, given up rock'n'roll and started again.

KEITH: We came off that tour not only full of confidence but knowing and learning shit it would take you years to pick up, by watching Don Peake, the Everly Brothers' guitarist, watching how they delivered things, watching how Little Richard would open a show, how he would swing the audience.

CHARLIE: Jim Gordon, the drummer with the Everly Brothers - he wrote 'Layla' with Eric - was the first American drummer I got close enough to watch. He was nineteen, I remember.

MICK: I used to spend a lot of time with Little Richard. He was very friendly and a great hero. He used to teach me a lot. I would watch him every single night to see how he handled the audience. He was a great audience manipulator, in the best sense of the word.

He had a fantastic show business understanding of the audience and how to get them at it, what numbers to play and when to quit. I probably learned more from him than anyone else.

KEITH: **Even at that age, nineteen or twenty, you'd wake up and slap your face saying "You're working with Little Richard and Bo Diddley".** Six months before we were thinking 'If only I could hear him one time'. And suddenly you're his friend and he goes "Pop round the pub, get me a drink, man". And Bo Diddley's asking me "Where the hell is Jerome Green?" - "I'll go get him, Bo". Suddenly it's a whole different trip.

MICK: There was another tour we did with John Leyton, who'd had a lot of hits. He was the headliner and then as the tour went on we were very lucky and we got these records, 'Not Fade Away' and 'I Wanna Be Your Man'. We became so popular on the tour that he had to give up being the headliner, which as you can imagine, was not very nice. But he was very, very gracious about it and very polite.

RON: It's no old wives' tale that I got Mick and Keith talking again on a few occasions, otherwise it was… hopeless. I'd get them on the phone, I'd make them ring me back and resolve it. I'd ring Mick and say "Look, I know where Keith is and he's ready to talk to you. Just ring him up and give me a ring back in 15 minutes or whenever you've finished talking". Sure enough Mick'd ring me back and say "He was ready". So on a lot of occasions it worked, but I stuck my neck out to keep the institution together, because I think it's worth it.

KEITH: Mick and I used to live very close, just down the street from each other, when we were about four or five, before we went to school. Up to 11 we went to the same school - Mick was in the year above, and we used to hang together. Then from 11 to 15, we went to different schools. He went to grammar school and they put me in the technical school… I mean, I'm the least technically-minded person in the world! So we split for a few years. I got expelled and went to Sidcup Art School. He went to the London School of Economics. It so happened that we just took the same train and he had all these American records, flash son of a bitch, because he comes from a better side of town from me. It's the music I'm trying to listen to. I've got a few singles, but he's got the bloody albums. I said "I can play that shit. I didn't know you were into that." Mick said "I've even got a little band". He was playing around Dartford doing Buddy Holly stuff, which is always a good beginning. I was just staring at the albums in his grasp. The Best Of Muddy Waters, Chuck Berry, Rocking At the Hop. I really wanted those albums, so I do it the nice way, say I'd like to have a listen one day. Ownership is nine points of the law, I mean. And he might reach the handle before I rob him of them.

BILL: WE HAD A KIND OF LITTLE OFFICE ON THE 1969 TOUR - THEY'D LIAISE WITH MICK - "WHAT TIME DO YOU WANT TO REHEARSE TOMORROW, MICK?" - AND MICK WOULD DO IT TO SUIT HIS PERSONAL DIARY. ✺ IF HE WAS PLAYING TENNIS IN THE AFTERNOON, HE'D SAY "IN THE EVENING" AND NOT CHECK WITH ANYBODY ELSE, WHICH WAS THE WAY HE WAS THEN. BUT THEN KEITH WOULDN'T TURN UP UNTIL THREE IN THE MORNING BECAUSE HE'D BEEN UP ALL NIGHT HANGING OUT WITH A FEW PEOPLE FROM ANOTHER BAND. ✺ THEN THE NEXT DAY THEY'D SAY "RIGHT, WE'VE GOT TO BE MORE CONSCIENTIOUS AND WE'LL START AT FIVE AND WORK TILL MIDNIGHT", AND MICK WOULDN'T TURN UP, HE'D GO OUT TO DINNER WITH SOME FRIENDS. ✺ MICK AND KEITH WOULD DO IT TO EACH OTHER. MICK WOULD BE ON TIME ONE NIGHT AND ANNOYED BECAUSE KEITH WASN'T THERE AND THEN KEITH WOULD FEEL GUILTY AND MAKE IT EARLY THE NEXT NIGHT AND MICK WOULD BE SO PISSED OFF WITH HIM FROM THE NIGHT BEFORE HE WOULDN'T TURN UP. ✺ THEY DID IT RIGHT THE WAY INTO THE 90S. IT WAS MADNESS, BUT THAT'S THE WAY THE BAND FUNCTIONED. IT SEEMED TO WORK: WE PRODUCED SOME MUSIC, ALTHOUGH I WOULDN'T ADVOCATE IT FOR OTHER BANDS.

MICK: I knew Keith from when I was a child, so I was always in touch with him. We used to play together because we lived very close by.

When he was about five years old he used to dress in a cowboy outfit - Roy Rogers, I think - with holsters and hat, and he had these big ears that stuck out.

I learnt that he played the guitar and we just went from there. We had a few friends in common who were all playing guitars. We were like 17 or something and we'd just play in people's back rooms… I don't think we really thought much about playing in public. I thought we were playing music which was a bit odd, because we started to play the blues. I kind of lost track of him because we went to different schools and then we saw each other on a train station. I had these records that I'd just bought from America. In those times they were so expensive. You couldn't buy them in England.

KEITH: The weirdest thing was that we were both very much into the same things, so that somewhere within us - despite all of our differences, which still exist - there was an intensity about what we liked and what we didn't like.

KEITH: There was always something between Brian, Mick and myself that didn't quite make it somewhere. Always something. I've often thought, tried to figure it out. It was in Brian, somewhere; there was something… He still felt alone somewhere… He was either completely into Mick at the expense of me, like nicking my bread to go and have a drink.

Or he'd be completely in with me trying to work something against Mick. Brian was a very weird cat. He was a little insecure. Maybe it was in the stars. He was a Pisces. I don't know. I'm Sag and Mick's a Leo. Maybe those three can't ever connect completely all together at the same time for very long. There were periods when we had a ball together.

CHARLIE: **I'm lucky to have been with these two. There's a magic about them that people like. They always argue, but they always love each other. They know each other so well. When I say they argue, they don't actually, but there's always a difference of opinion. They're two totally different people. One is meticulous and detailed, and the other is a complete bohemian. But they both have a direction for themselves and they can both see whatever it is - I'm fortunate to be in there as part of that.**

KEITH: JUST SITTING IN THAT TRAIN CARRIAGE IN DARTFORD, IT WAS ALMOST LIKE WE MADE A DEAL WITHOUT KNOWING IT. LIKE ROBERT JOHNSON AT THE CROSSROADS. I DON'T KNOW WHY IT SHOULD HAVE HAPPENED, BUT THERE WAS A BOND MADE THERE THAT DESPITE EVERYTHING ELSE GOES ON AND ON - LIKE A SOLID DEAL.

KEITH: **It was Andrew who pointed out to us that if we didn't start finding a source of new material this thing wouldn't last. How long could you cover other people's - how many obscure great songs are you going to find? So for me the greatest contribution Andrew ever made was to lock me and Mick in the kitchen for a day and night and say "I'm not letting you out until you've got a song". Mick and I learnt very quickly in retrospect. It seemed a long time at the time until we were able to say "Do we have the balls to give this to the rest of the boys to play" - until we came up with 'The Last Time'.**

BILL: **America** was where all our music came from and there was the magical thought of going there with all the radio stations and being able to find all the records you wanted.

MICK: **America** was very difficult.

The Beatles had already been but they were not successful on the first trip. Nobody really took to them. You won't read that, actually. They hadn't had a hit, and America's a very large country, so it's hard to break the first time.

BILL: We really went there as a three-week promotion thing, a few gigs, TV, radio. The whole of America then was like the mid-West. We were so bizarre for them to deal with at the time, although we didn't think so, and we didn't understand the reaction. The clothes we wore and the hair thing - because they were all crew-cut, that was the style. We got it from every direction, morning, noon and night. You know, people shouting "Are you girls?", "Are you the Beatles?"; they'd swear at you and abuse you. Everybody that talked to you on the radio said sarcastic things like "You could see the fleas jumping off their heads" and "They smelled". It was what you realise black people have had to deal with for many, many years.

KEITH: First time in Omaha in 64. Drinking whiskey and Coke out of cups, paper cups, just waiting to go on. Cops walked in. "What's that?" "Whiskey". "You can't drink whiskey in a public place." I happened to be drinking just Coke actually. "Tip it down the bog". I said "No man, I've just got Coca-Cola in here". I look up and I got a .44 lookin' at me, right between the eyes.

BILL: We had to fly to San Antonio, Texas, because GAC had put us into these weird places to play. The gig was at the Texas State Fair, a rodeo-cum-music thing. It was really bizarre, the wrong audience and everything. Then we went to LA and did television, the Hollywood Palace show, which was like second in line to the Ed Sullivan show, which we couldn't get on. And we just got totally ridiculed, live on television, by Dean Martin. He was the compere and drunk out of his brain anyway. He was just fucking rude, which didn't do us any good. And they cut our three songs to 45 seconds of one song, that's all we got. It was a total disaster.

DEAN MARTIN: **The Rolling Stones, aren't they great? Well I'm going to let you in on something. You know these singing groups today, you're under the impression they have long hair. Not true at all. It's an optical illusion: they just have low foreheads and high eyebrows.**

KEITH: If Dino had thought a little more, he wouldn't have been quite so flippant, but then I don't blame him. At the time it was like a deadly insult, but all those things only went to make us want to prove ourselves so that we could come back and bite your head off.

MICK: I really don't know what's considered rude in America 'cause it's all so different, isn't it! Here you can use Americanisms and people don't know what you're saying. Censorship is weird. 1968

MICK: THE FIRST TOUR WAS TOUGH. WE WERE POPULAR IN NEW YORK, POPULAR IN LA, THE BITS ON THE EDGES, BUT THERE'S THE BIG BIT IN THE MIDDLE WHERE NO ONE KNOWS YOU AND WE USED TO PLAY EMPTY STADIUMS. THE GOOD THING WAS THE BEATLES HAD DONE THIS BEFORE SO WE DIDN'T HAVE TO GO IN THERE FIRST.

KEITH: THE FIRST GIG WAS IN SAN BERNADINO. IT WAS A STRAIGHT GAS, MAN.

BILL: We did one wonderful gig. San Bernadino, California. They knew about us in California for some reason, I don't know why. There were 400 kids packed into a small open air place and they went fucking nuts. Exactly like they did in England. Police on the stage fighting them and the kids were stampeding the stage. An absolutely wonderful show. Then we did six or seven weird shows all the way up America and ended up at Carnegie Hall in New York. We did two shows there, bedlam, the same thing. They tried to cancel the second show in New York: the kids on stage, screaming. So we actually broke California and New York in a way, even if it was in a small way. We lost money, but it was worth it.

CHARLIE: I went to every single jazz club. I remember going to Birdland and seeing Charlie Mingus with his 13-piece orchestra. That to me was America - the rest I didn't give a shit about. I didn't know anything about the place.

MICK: We had two successful gigs in LA and New York. On the documentary stuff the Carnegie Hall gig looks like England, you could be in Liverpool. All girls in black, very young: they'd got this underground thing going.

CHARLIE: Carnegie Hall was fantastic. Me and Stu sitting there - it was like Gene Krupa and Benny Goodman. All that history. A bit like going into the Long Room at Lords and thinking 'I can't believe I'm here along with all the others who've been here before'. I like that sort of thing.

BILL: We did a second tour of the States in October and November 64, and that was better: better organised, better gigs. I think we had Patti Labelle and the Bluebells, the Vibrations and the Standells. We still lost money, but we played Chicago and places like that. We recorded in Chicago at Chess, met Chuck Berry, Muddy Waters, Willie Dixon, Buddy Guy, and they all liked what we were doing because we were playing their kind of music. We did the first Ed Sullivan show on that tour, and the TAMI Show as well. They put us top of the bill above James Brown - we had to follow him: that was a nightmare. But it was good for us because it got us seen and known. And we travelled in a bus - our first tour in a bus, because we didn't even do that in England...

CHARLIE: We did some dreadful things with people I'd never ever met before. They were called disc jockeys of the old school, in other words Murray the K - he was bloody barmy, this being I'd never met the likes of, a maniac, completely over the top of everything. The first time I met him I walked out of the studio, I couldn't take it.

KEITH: Ah, Murray. The fifth Beatle and the sixth Rolling Stone. Nobody realises how America blew our minds and the Beatles too. Can't even describe what America meant to us. We first started listening to Otis when we got to the States, and picked up our first Stax singles. And Wilson Pickett. That's what's so amazing about Bobby Keys, that cat, man, he was there from the beginning.

BILL: July and August 1964 were probably the two most horrendous months of our career. Every gig we did was stopped by the police with crowds on the stage. At Blackpool there was no protection, no security anywhere, 6000 people in this huge ballroom. It was Scots weekend and they were all down from Glasgow getting drunk. There were about 30 guys forcing their way through the crowd. You could see them coming. They just lined up all along the front of the stage, which was quite high, about five feet, and they had their heads and arms resting on the stage. They decided to spit at us, taking turns who could hit who. Keith got a bit pissed off with it after a while and he said to one guy who'd just spat at him "You do that again and I'll fucking kill you". The guy did, and Keith ran across the stage and used his head as a football, smack, kicked him right in the face. Mayhem. They all went nuts and we dropped everything and jumped the drums. They took a full-sized piano and threw it off stage, smashed it into shreds, a fucking grand piano, they didn't mess about.

KEITH: In those days I had a temper. I shouted "You spit on me?" and I kicked his face in.

MICK: They were being kind of lairy and Keith booted someone and then it was just mayhem. That was an extreme case. They smashed everything up, very violent. I mean, it was nothing to do with us really. We were just the catalyst.

CHARLIE: That was a classic. It was completely packed. This guy down the front was pissed as a newt, as most of us were, and then he started spitting at Keith. Keith kicked his head, just like a football. It went boom! When they dropped that beautiful white Steinway off the stage, Stu was in tears.

BILL: Stu arrived about two or three in the morning. He walked into the lounge of this little hotel where we were sitting having coffee and he had a ragged bit of wood with a bit of bent metal and he said "That's your amp, and that's what's left of your guitar". He had this collection of scraps of stuff and passed them out to each member of the band.

CHARLIE: I was with Keith, and Stu came in with this corner of an amplifier, the plywood hanging off it, and he went "There we are, kiddies". Typical Stu, that was.

BILL: The same thing happened in this beautiful old opera house in the Hague. They just ripped the place to pieces. We were on stage for seven minutes. One number at full volume, and two with no electricity. All the power got switched off by the cops. We tried to carry on with maracas and tambourines but we just had to give up. The police made us leave and then the audience destroyed the place, pulled the tapestries off the walls, ripped the fitted chairs out and threw them into the chandeliers. It was really awful.

CHARLIE: Stu was hit on the head with a bottle, very badly - it caught his eye. I had the usual things, because you can't get out of the way if you're a drummer. That was the period where they threw coins at you: they're really awful projectiles.

BILL: I wouldn't say it was frightening, it was sort of amusing in a way. We used to laugh and think it was quite funny, especially Brian and Keith, who were a bit sick in their humour. They got a lot of fun out of it.

KEITH: You're like twenty years old and every little chick in all of fucking England seems to think you're fucking Rudolph Valentino. It's mind-boggling. You can't hear yourself play, you almost give up playing. We used to play 'Popeye The Sailor Man' - they never knew the difference. You couldn't get louder than the screaming. Chicks were throwing themselves off the balcony onto the seats below. It's amazing that nobody actually died - I think there were a few broken ribs and shoulders.

TONY KING: The first time I saw them was in the Scene Club in Ham Yard in 1963 with Chrissie Shrimpton, who was Mick's girlfriend. She said "Come and see my boyfriend, he's in a really good band". I thought they were a bit of an unruly mob. A bit louder and lairier than the Beatles.

KEITH: Our main aim through 1964 was not what we were going to play, but how we were going to get out. You had the Chief Inspector of Leicester or somewhere leading you over the roofs. He'd have his uniform and three or four of his trusted constables and we're all stuck up on this fucking roof for hours surrounded by teens who've spotted him in his uniform and know what's going on.

BILL: In 1963 and 1964 we played more than anybody else has ever played, I think, it was stated in one of the pop magazines. In one of those years we played 360 of the 365 days. We really worked our balls off. We had no time off. I don't know where Keith and Mick found the time to write songs.

KEITH: We worked our asses off from 63 to 66, right through those three years, non-stop. I believe we had two weeks off. That's nothing. I mean, I tell that to B.B. King and he'll say "I've been doing it for years".

BILL: We were high quality players on stage. I'm not one for bragging, but we were the best live band in England, and remained the best, probably for 15 years. There was just something that happened when we were on stage. Everybody knew exactly what was going to happen. Even if somebody made a mistake everybody else did it with them, like ESP. We were totally in tune musically and in our heads. And Mick was a fantastic performer on stage; there was no one better.

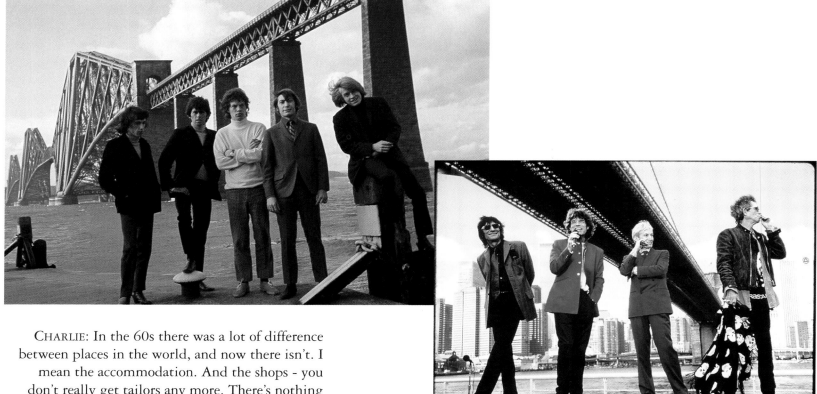

CHARLIE: In the 60s there was a lot of difference between places in the world, and now there isn't. I mean the accommodation. And the shops - you don't really get tailors any more. There's nothing worse than shopping malls. Voodoo Lounge was my shopping mall tour and I've never been to one since.

MICHAEL COHL: In 1990 we went to Tokyo: that was the first time the Rolling Stones had ever played there. In 1995 we went to South America and the Rolling Stones hadn't played there as a touring entity. It was like the 60s - unbelievable. We got to the hotel in Buenos Aires and there were 5,000 people surrounding the building. We had to fight our way in. They sat on the street with guitars and sang Rolling Stones songs all night. It was aggravating, but it was awesome.

CHARLIE: The French have always liked us, or Mick, or whatever -they still do. And for some reason typically French. They were the only country in the world that never thought the Beatles were as big as America thought they were.

MICK: We went to France eventually and did a show at the Olympia where the Beatles had done very badly. They did a very unsuccessful series of shows with a terrible bill. Typically French, you know, they knew that everyone loved the Beatles, so they didn't. And we did this series of shows at the Olympia which was great.

BILL: I remember a night, well a day and a night, when we had to go to Lowestoft to play. In those days there wasn't a motorway, so it took forever to get there. Because of all those little roads, it must have taken us four hours. And the next night we were playing in Aberystwyth in Wales. We left Lowestoft in the morning and we were in the van the entire day, never stopped for food, maybe for a wee on a couple of occasions. We finally arrived in Aberystwyth about an hour before the gig. We played, left and drove again to Birmingham to do the next day's Thank Your Lucky Stars. We didn't sleep or eat again. We arrived at the studios about seven in the morning and they wouldn't let us in. They said "You're not supposed to be here", but we begged and pleaded and in the end we got in this little viewing room somewhere, laid on the floor and crashed till 11 or something.

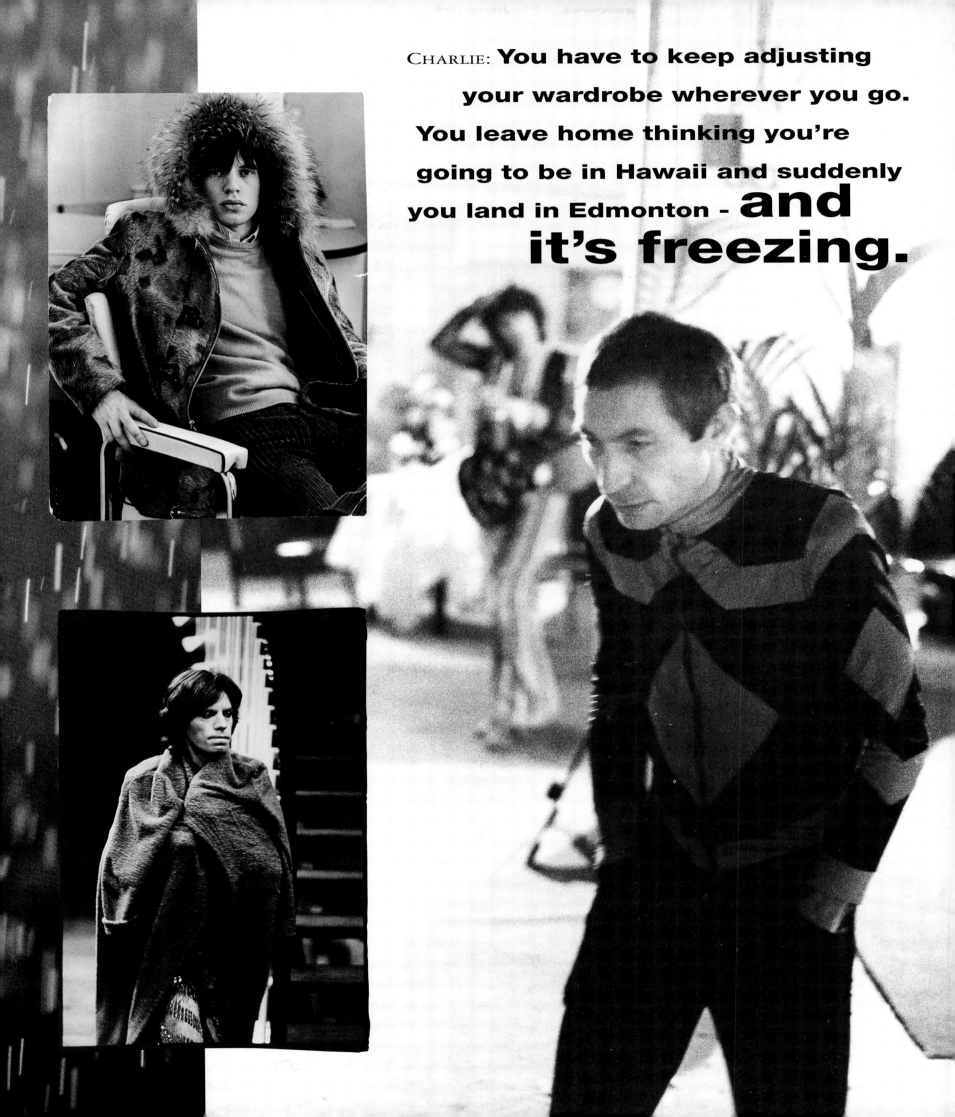

CHARLIE: **You have to keep adjusting your wardrobe wherever you go. You leave home thinking you're going to be in Hawaii and suddenly you land in Edmonton - and it's freezing.**

BILL: ABOUT A WEEK BEFORE THE ROMFORD INCIDENT WE DID SOME TV IN BIRMINGHAM AND ON THE WAY BACK IN THE SUBURBS I SAID "I'VE GOT TO GO TO THE TOILET. STOP STU, ANYWHERE, I DON'T CARE BUT I'VE JUST GOT TO GO". HE DROVE FOR A WHILE AND I SAID "LOOK, YOU'VE GOT TO STOP BECAUSE OTHERWISE I'M JUST GOING TO GO", SO HE PULLED UP IN THIS TREE-LINED SIDE STREET, AND I WENT OVER TO THIS FENCE. 👅 WHILE I'M WEEING UP AGAINST IT I GET A TORCH SHONE ON ME AND THE USUAL "HELLO, HELLO, WHAT'S GOING ON HERE?" I TOLD THIS POLICEMAN WE'D JUST COME FROM THE TV STUDIO ETC. ETC. AND HE SAID "I'LL LET YOU OFF THIS TIME, BUT DON'T EVER DO IT AGAIN". AND WE GOT IN THE VAN AND WENT HOME. 👅 A WEEK LATER THE SAME THING HAPPENED. I SAID "I'VE GOT TO GO", SO STU PULLED UP AT THIS GARAGE ON THE MAIN STREET IN STRATFORD AND I GOT OUT, WENT OVER TO THE GUY AND SAID "EXCUSE ME, HAVE YOU GOT A TOILET I CAN USE?" AND HE SAID "NO, GO AWAY, GET OFF MY FORECOURT" OR SOMETHING LIKE THAT. SO I WENT BACK TO THE VAN AND I'M BURSTING. AND MICK SAID "COME ON BILL, WE'LL FIND YOU A TOILET", SO HE AND BRIAN GOT OUT WITH A FRIEND OF OURS, JOEY PAIGE, THE EVERLY BROTHERS' BASS PLAYER, AND WE WENT BACK AND THEN THE GUY GOT REALLY PANICKY AND ANGRY. 👅 BRIAN STARTED DOING HIS NANKER FACE, HIM AND KEITH DANCING ROUND GOING

"Get off my foreskin,

AND WE WERE HAVING GOES AT HIM. SO WE LEFT THE FORECOURT, WENT DOWN A SIDE STREET, PEED AGAINST THE WALL AND THAT WAS THE END OF IT. 👅 THE NEXT DAY WE'RE SUMMONSED BY THE POLICE: THEY PUT A REPORT IN SAYING WE'VE BEEN PISSING ALL OVER THE GARAGE, TOTALLY UNTRUE. WE HAD TO GO TO COURT, ACCUSED OF ALL THINGS WE DIDN'T DO, ABUSIVE BEHAVIOUR, OBSCENE LANGUAGE, URINATING IN FULL VIEW. 👅 WE GOT FOUND GUILTY, AND FINED £6.00 EACH WITH £25.00 COSTS, AND THEN WE STOOD BACK AND THOUGHT "WE'VE BEEN IN THE PAPER FOR TWO WEEKS, FRONT PAGE, AND IT COST US ABOUT £50.00". IT WAS GREAT PUBLICITY.

MICK: We just parked the van, got the petrol, asked the bloke for the loo.
He said there wasn't one so we just went anyway. Very discreetly, but of course it was huge.
Can you imagine getting caught for that?

get off my foreskin"

KEITH: Travelling in the Volkswagen **you got really adept at pissing through the air vents.** You had to stand on the engine beam and get your cock out. Stu wasn't gonna stop for anything. He'd **say** "If I stop for **you** lot to take a pee we'll never see the fucking gig".

KEITH: Sometimes we'd be stuck way out of town and the cops would say "You can't stay in the city, you're going to jam up the traffic". So there were all these chicks waiting to get laid and you're 15-20 miles out of town, which in the 60s was a long way - not so many cars as there are now.

CHARLIE: I bloody hated it personally. They'd chase you in cake shops and things. It's wonderful to go on with an audience like that, and that sort of noise, but I never liked not being able to go out properly, ie walk downstairs and go out the front door. I hate that. I still do actually - I never see what all the fuss is about. Mick gets it worse than I do...

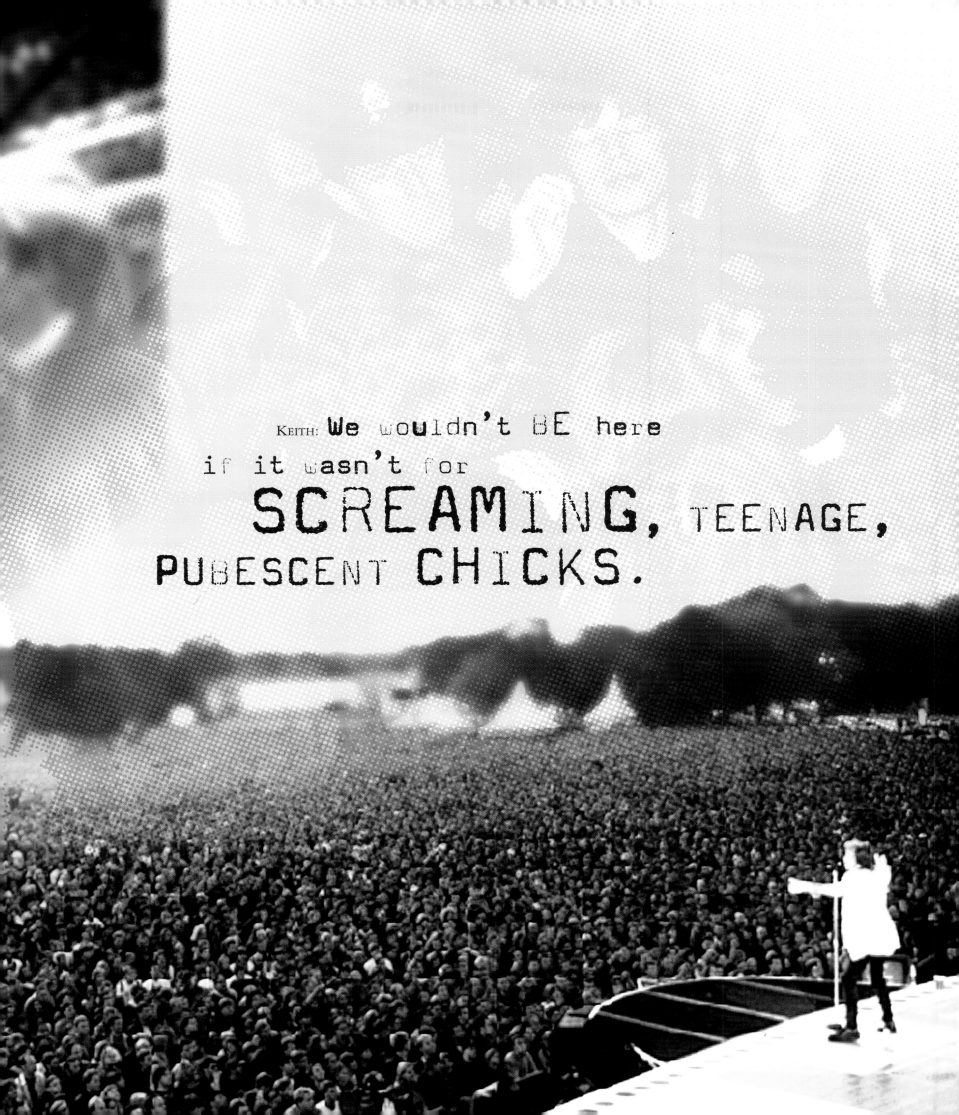

KEITH: We wouldn't BE here
if it wasn't for
SCREAMING, TEENAGE,
PUBESCENT CHICKS.

BILL: At the beginning we played such different music that the kids didn't really know what to do with us, so we didn't have the girl adulation then. The screaming started after we'd done a couple more TV shows and the tour with the Everlys and Bo Diddley.

KEITH: I got strangled twice. That's why I never wear anything around my neck anymore. Going out of theatres was the dodgiest. One chick grabs one side of the chain and another chick grabs the other side… Another time I found myself lying in the gutter with shirt on and half a pair of pants and the car roaring away down the street. Oh shit, man. They leap on you. "What do you want? What?" 1971

MICK: There'd been girls screaming for a long time. You couldn't hear anything because the amps or the PA weren't big enough. We were quite a serious band in our way. We used to think 'We're not like these rock bands in sparkly jackets. We're serious. We've got nuances, we know about the history of the music, we've got hit records with slide guitars on them, we're doing Bo Diddley beat records and making them into hits. We're serious but we're not able to play now'. It had become a bit of a joke, not very satisfying from a performance point of view.

TONY KING: There were always lots of dopey girls standing outside the office who'd say they were going to commit suicide if Mick didn't kiss them. He'd sort of not kiss them - one of them called up and said she'd taken an overdose of Pro-Plus, and we all laughed in the office. And then one of them called Marilyn managed to get her tongue down Mick's throat one day when he walked in, and he said "Oh my God, that was disgusting".

BILL: It was mad. People were jumping off balconies up in the gods down into the crowds and breaking their arms and jaws. There were people diving in front of the cars, getting their fingers ripped off in the windscreen wipers as we drove away, people climbing under the van and holding on to the bloody driveshaft. People would climb up hotel fire escapes, drainpipes, hide in the rooms. It just got impossible. The Beatles were going through exactly the same thing on a different level, and they had to stop touring and we had to at almost exactly the same time.

BOBBY KEYS: People listen more now. People out there are paying a hell of a lot more money. We draw an older crowd, you know, you don't see the panties and the bras and the other stuff flying up on stage like you used to. The odd one will come up, though.

KEITH: FOR ABOUT TWO YEARS WE LEARNT HOW TO RUN.
THE GETAWAY WAS THE ONLY THING WE WORKED UPON ALL DAY. IT WAS "HOW ARE WE GOING TO GET OUT OF THERE BECAUSE WE KNOW IT'S GOING TO BE A RIOT".

MICK: **It's kind of attractive for a very young man to have all this attention and flattery and girls chasing you down the street. I think we all enjoyed it - up to a point. You get used to getting your clothes ripped and pulled. But it was a bit scary.**

TONY KING: **The first thing you do when you get into the hotel room is clear away all the complimentary magazines because surface space becomes very valuable. And then you look at the rooming list to see if you're near Ronnie or Keith. Because that means noise. I was opposite Ronnie once and as soon as we'd checked into the hotel - because we were there for six days - I went down to the lobby and said "Could I be moved, please, because I'm right opposite the party room".**

MICK: I used to share with Keith sometimes but I also shared with Charlie. I never shared with Brian. And Bill refused to share.

BILL: Brian and me used to share all the time. Stu was quite good, he used to pick these little hotels in the country, motel-type hotels. We used to have two bedrooms and a sitting room. It was mostly me and Brian sharing. Charlie was married: Shirley would be on the phone all night from Australia or wherever. Mick and Keith used to be hanging out writing songs, they didn't go out much at all. Me and Brian would go out, do the town, pull girls and have fun.

KEITH: The first thing you need to do with a hotel room is to stop it looking like a hotel room. It's a mini stage, right? I carry my own stereo. If I'm on the road for a year or so and I've got to be listening to stuff, I can't keep listening to it on different stereos everywhere I go. So my big luxury is carrying a big stereo - about three Samsonite cases full of sound. I couldn't live without that cushion of sound.

ALAN DUNN: We stopped on the island of Bali on the way back from Australia. It wasn't anywhere near as commercialised as it is now. There was a lovely hotel, and the Duke and Duchess of Bedford had been there just before. When we came to leave, the owner said "You'll have to excuse the room being a bit sparse and bare, but the Duke and Duchess told me that you smashed up hotel rooms". So they'd cleared everything out. All the knick-knacks and ornaments had been removed.

TONY KING: It's like a king used to travel in England - announcing to some poor unsuspecting householder in Derbyshire that he was descending with his court and they had to clear everything out to make room for him and his courtiers. We descend on the Ritz Carlton or the Four Seasons and all the best suites are taken by us and we have security people on the floors and we arrive at night. The poor hotel has to undergo a siege for the next few days.

ALAN DUNN: On the curbside when we pull up there's about 250 pieces and they charge you to take every piece up to the rooms. So it's $1000 in and $1000 out.

MICHAEL COHL: The hotels are used to us now. We're not the only rock band - we stay in a hotel and ten other groups have stayed at the same place.

JIM CALLAGHAN: We used to have this support band - Toots and the Maytals - and Keith was having one of his parties, which he had every night, and they'd come up and party with him… they left the next afternoon and he was still partying with whoever. the next evening they were back and he was partying for three days, and we were going "Oh"… That was how it was up to 1977 or whenever.

KEITH: After a show the wise man will take it easy, digest his food, then put himself to bed. But then there might be a knock at the door and somebody would come in and say "You've got to see this, this is great", and suddenly there's ten people in the room and somebody's got a great video or record to play, and before you know it there's a party in full swing.

AND THEN, WOULD THE WISE MAN REALLY WANT TO FOREGO A GOOD PARTY?

CHARLIE: I MAKE A SKETCH OF EVERY BEDROOM I SLEEP IN. IF YOU'RE IN A PLACE FOR TWO OR THREE DAYS, IT'S COMFORTABLE TO COMPLETE. WHEN YOU'RE IN AND OUT IT'S HARD, BUT I'VE SKETCHED EVERY BED I'VE SLEPT IN ON TOUR SINCE ABOUT 1968. IT'S A VISUAL DIARY THAT DOESN'T MEAN ANYTHING TO ANYONE. I NEVER LOOK THROUGH THEM ONCE I'VE DONE THEM, TO BE HONEST. IT'S MORE A RECORD, TO KNOW I'VE GOT IT... I'LL LOOK AT THEM ALL ONE DAY.

CHARLIE: Mick has one of those minds and bums.

His bum won't sit still and his mind doesn't either.

It's always onwards, onwards, onwards - like yesterday is history already. So it's very difficult for him to keep his interest in a band that is so steeped in history - at least, that's my slant on him.

RON: Mick does a lot of research. I remember him giving advice back in 1975 to Steve Tyler, I think, when Aerosmith were going to play Australia and Mick was saying "Make sure if you're doing the mid-day show you must have a canopy over the stage, otherwise you'll roast because it gets so boiling", little tips like that. And he would always go to a new venue and watch someone play there. You'd see Mick in the gods, just checking out the sound.

CHARLIE: Mick is probably the best thing live on stage. He very rarely stands there and sings a song. He performs every song. James Brown was the same: he would sing immaculately and perform every song with a bit of show in the middle of it. Mick learned a lot of that off people like Brown - it's from a very old school.

BERNARD FOWLER: I'm looking out for Mick constantly because I have to sing a lot of parts with him, so if I'm not watching him I'll fuck it up. He can't fuck it up - he's always right, even when he's wrong he's right.

KEITH: NO MATTER HOW YOU FEEL ABOUT A GIG, FROM THE BAND'S POINT OF VIEW IT'S TO SUPPORT THE MAN IN FRONT. THERE'S NO POINT IN DOING IT OTHERWISE. IF YOU'RE THERE TO CHOP HIM DOWN, IF YOU'RE NOT THERE TO SUPPORT, THEN YOU'RE NOT A BAND.

MY JOB WITH THE STONES IS BEING A SAFETY NET FOR MICK, NEVER HAVING TO WORRY IF HE COULDN'T HEAR ANYTHING OUT ON THE LEFT OR THE RIGHT OR WHEREVER HE WAS - HE COULD SCREW IT UP AND WE'D TURN THE BEAT ROUND AND CATCH HIM.

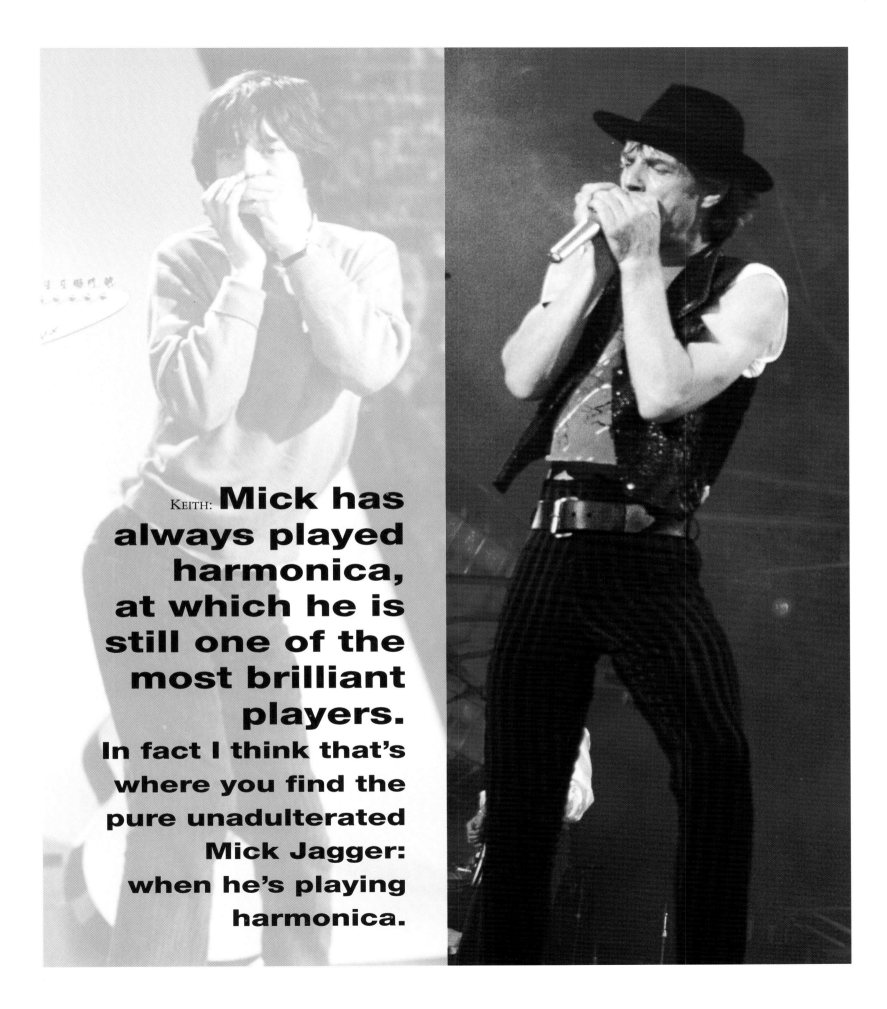

KEITH: **Mick has always played harmonica, at which he is still one of the most brilliant players. In fact I think that's where you find the pure unadulterated Mick Jagger: when he's playing harmonica.**

KEITH: Warsaw in 67. We get there, behind the Iron Curtain, do the whole bit, all very uptight. There's Army at the airport. Get to the hotel which is very jail-like. We're invited by the Minister of Culture, on a cultural visit, and we're playing in the Palace of Culture. We get there to do our gig. We go on…

"Honksi-de-boyski, boysk. Zee Rolling Stones-ki".

And who's got the best seats in the house right down front? The sons and daughters of the Communist Party. They're sitting there with their diamonds and their pearls. And their fingers in their ears.

About three numbers, and I say "Fuckin' stop playin' Charlie. You fuckin' lot, get out and let those bastards in the back down front". So they went. About four rows just walked out. All the momma and daddy's boys. Outside, they've got water cannons…

BILL: We had another madness in Greece in early 67. They put us in the Parathanikos Football Stadium, with the crowds in seats and three rows of police, so they weren't allowed to leave the seats. Of course as soon as we started they all poured onto the pitch, running and tackling the cops and they stopped the show about three times. And the police were beating them with batons, really viciously. Tom Keylock was with us because he worked for Keith and we had all these big bunches of flowers we were going to distribute but we couldn't get them to the crowd. So Keylock says "I'll do it". He took two armfuls and jumped off stage and ran and had a fight with the police; they broke his nose or wrist. The rest all left for England, while I stayed for a holiday and got stuck there, because two days later there was the military coup - that's probably why the police were so uptight. And then we didn't tour until Hyde Park and America in 1969.

KEITH: "Bang, bang, bang". There's this big knock at the door and I go to answer it. "Oh look, there's lots of little ladies and gentlemen outside." He says "Read this", and I'm goin' "Whaa, whaa? All right". When it came down to it, they couldn't pin anything at all on us. All they could pin on me was allowing people to smoke on my premises. All they could pin on Mick was these four amphetamine tablets that he'd bought in Italy across the counter. They don't like young kids with a lot of money. But as long as you don't bother them, that's cool. But we bothered them. We bothered 'em because of the way we looked, the way we'd act. Because we never showed any reverence for them whatsoever.

MICK: After the arrests touring was much more difficult. I think we couldn't get visas to America for a long time, until 1969. But the rest of the world, apart from Japan, which we'd never been to, and as far as I know we'd never been asked to go to, was all right. But I never thought that there were people watching me.

CHARLIE: When Mick and Keith got nicked they were put in prison in Lewes, which is just up the road from where I live. We couldn't go and visit: it wasn't a good idea apparently. I don't think it affected the public, probably because of the image we had. It's not something you approve of, but at the time it was rather avant-garde, it was new to have young stars in England, so people went along with it.

MICK: ONCE YOU GET IN TROUBLE WITH THE POLICE, YOU'RE ALWAYS IN TROUBLE AND THAT'S IT. THEY SHOULD BE LOOKING AFTER PEOPLE AND TURNING AMERICAN TOURISTS AWAY FROM PICCADILLY CIRCUS. 1968

BILL: I cheated. I told the others I got car sick if I went in the back, so they let me go in the front for three years until they tumbled me - I never got in the front again. I was in the back forever. The black hole of Calcutta, we used to call it.

BILL: In December 1962 we went to a gig in Putney, before Charlie joined actually, and we went on the fucking bus from Chelsea with all the gear all the amps, the guitars, the drums, everything and we had an enormous row with the conductor. He wasn't going to let us on. In the end, I don't know why, he relented, but I don't know how we got back. Even before that Tony Chapman used to bring his drums to our gigs on his Mum's bicycle. You didn't have transport. People didn't have cars. Then Stu managed to get some shares from ICI, where he worked. He sold them and bought a van, a Commer or something.

KEITH: It didn't matter if you were going to London, Manchester, Newcastle, Exeter, Penzance, Weston-super-Mare, Bill sat up the front with Stu comfy and we were in the back with one window at the back and two little air vents. You try going from Lowestoft to Aberystwyth, try going East to West - all the roads went North and South and it went on and on. You got to know England fairly intimately, but it was a weird, distorted view of it through a back window and those little gills.

CHARLIE: Bill used to complain of stomach aches so he was permanently in the front seat. Keith and I used to sleep on the back ledge, freezing cold. It's a wonder we never got lice or anything. I remember Keith and those Beatle boots of his with the ends sticking up by my head.

MICK: Bill always bagged the front seat, the only seat in the van.

KEITH: ## IT WAS A PERSONALISED HELL. PRISON IS EASY AFTER THAT. STU WAS THE WARDEN AND HE WAS MERCILESS.

BILL: If you went round a corner sharp, the whole lot came down on top of you. In fact we had to dig Keith out once because all the stuff came down on top of him. He was knocked out for a while.

CHARLIE: Stu was never that careful a person with anybody so he'd turn corners and the whole lot of you and the drums would move. We used to have a chair which would move as well. That was the worst spot I thought, like being the gunner in a Wellington bomber. It never stayed still.

ALAN DUNN: In the early days we'd somehow get hold of a brand-new van, the worst thing you could do: they weren't too reliable. We'd drive through the night and come to a border and I'd push all my hair up into my hat because it was quite long and the border guards still had this thing about long-haired hippie travellers. At one border the guy made me take my hat off and that was it. Everything out of the back, all the equipment out, and Ian's going "Bloody Germans…That's why I never got bananas until I was eight because of them…"

ALAN DUNN: IT'S A CUSTOMISED BOEING 727 WHICH NORMALLY WOULD HAVE 200 SEATS BUT HAS BEEN CUSTOMISED DOWN TO 59 SEATS, FOUR VERY PRIVATE COMPARTMENTS AND A BIG LUXURY BAR. ALL THE REST IS FIRST-CLASS SEATING, SLEEPER SEATS.

NOT
THAT
ANYBODY
EVER
SLEEPS.

KEITH: THERE WAS A TIME IN 67, WHEN EVERYBODY JUST STOPPED, EVERYTHING **JUST STOPPED DEAD.** EVERYBODY WAS TRYING TO WORK IT OUT, WHAT WAS GOING TO GO ON. SO MANY WEIRD THINGS HAPPENING TO SO MANY WEIRD PEOPLE AT ONE TIME.

MICK: I'd like to perform and I think the Stones would, but we're stuck because we feel it's no good having everybody sit down and be quiet. I don't want anybody to have to do anything. 1968

CHARLIE: I think we were tired and there was a lifestyle that Mick and Keith had going. They had made some money and hadn't seen any of the world so they'd go to Morocco or wherever. In fact that's exactly what Brian and Keith did - went to Morocco together. They came back different people I think. Keith came back better, Brian I don't think so because he wasn't strong enough to take any abuse to himself.

MICK **That was a very difficult period. The drugs, the brawls, the internal squabbling. It's hard to recreate.**

It was a difficult time in society, you had a lot of people going against you, authority figures. You were supposed to live up to some sort of reputation, always defending it.

BOBBY KEYS: We were going through the Mont Blanc tunnel and we got snowed in. There was a little bed and breakfast place, and this beautiful barmaid. She didn't speak a word of English and I didn't speak a word of anything but Texan. So somehow through hand gestures and nods and winks and smiles she eventually came back to my room to listen to the next Rolling Stones album. Romance was in the air, what can I say? And I was trying to think 'How the hell can I impress this lady?' and somewhere in the back of my memory I'd heard something about champagne baths and I thought 'I wonder how she'll react to that'. I thought French stuff was probably five bucks a quart - thought I'd spend about a couple of hundred dollars.

But it was all Dom Perignon. Takes a lot to fill a bath up…

It was a rollicking success… And on the flight they came up to me and said "We hope you're not planning on any profit for the rest of this tour". I said "What are you talking about?" - "Well, there's a little bill here we've received for some large amount of champagne". I said "Oh man, no, no, that'll be a mistake…" But, you know, I've never regretted it.

BILL: BRIAN AND KEITH HAD SOME HORRENDOUS GAMES

AND THEY WERE REALLY SICK. WE WERE ALL GIVEN RUSSIAN MOVIE CAMERAS ONCE AS A SPONSORSHIP AND THEY SPENT THEIR TIME TAKING MOVIES OF PEOPLE IN WHEEL-CHAIRS, THAT'S ALL THEY TOOK PHOTOS OF. AND THEY USED TO HAVE DIFFERENT NAMES FOR DIFFERENT KINDS OF SNOT: GREEN GILBERTS AND YELLOW HUMPHRIES AND POLKADOT PERKINS. THEY USED TO BE ON THE WALL IN THE FLAT. THEY'D THINK UP LOONY THINGS WHEN THEY WERE IN BED ALL DAY WHEN THEY WERE FREEZING AND STARVING IN THE WINTER OF 1963 AND 64.

CHARLIE:
I'D NEVER HEARD A GUY PLAY AS GOOD A BOTTLENECK AS BRIAN,

EXCEPT GEOFF BRADFORD, OF COURSE, BUT GEOFF WAS MUCH MORE FOLKY, MORE OF A PURIST IN HIS PLAYING. BRIAN WAS MORE OF AN ELMORE JAMES, RAW - IT WAS GREAT AND NOBODY HAD HEARD THAT BEFORE.

KEITH: Alexis Korner goes up and says "We got a guest to play some guitar. He comes from Cheltenham. All the way from Cheltenham just to play for ya". Suddenly, it's Elmore James, this cat, man. And it's Brian, man... He's bent over... Da-da-da, da-da-da... I said "What? What the fuck?" Playing bar slide guitar. We get into Brian after he finishes 'Dust My Blues'. He's really fantastic and a gas. He'd been doing the same as we'd been doing... Thinking he was the only cat in the world who was doing it.

CHARLIE: I think what happened with Brian was that Mick and Keith's writing took off. Brian was the band's catalyst really, the one who did all the work of getting the thing together. And slowly Mick was the one people were looking at. When we first started Brian was the one they used to scream at, but then Mick became bigger - he became very good at what he did, and Keith became very good at what he was doing and Brian just became a parody of Brian in the end. He'd do these strange movements on stage, but they were him doing Brian. Gradually he got left behind. To be honest I was not really aware of it at the time.

KEITH: Brian would go out and meet a lot of people, before we did, because Mick and I spent most of our time writing. He'd go out and get high somewhere, get smashed. We'd say, "Look, we got a session tomorrow, man, got to keep it together". He'd come, completely out of his head, and zonk out on the floor with his guitar over him. So we started overdubbing, which was a drag 'cause it meant the whole band wasn't playing.

BILL: BRIAN GOT SICK QUITE A LOT ON TOUR AND DIDN'T TURN UP FOR GIGS. WE OFTEN PLAYED WITHOUT HIM, JUST THE FOUR OF US. STU WOULD SIT IN ON PIANO SOMETIMES AND WE'D MIKE HIM UP TO FILL OUT THE SOUND A BIT. ON THE SECOND TOUR OF AMERICA WE PLAYED TEN DAYS WITHOUT BRIAN, AND HE FINALLY TURNED UP ON THE LAST GIG. HE WAS NOT THAT WELL. HE WAS ONE OF THOSE PEOPLE THAT ARE A BIT OF A HYPOCHONDRIAC AND ALSO A BIT OF A WORRIER. HE WAS HIGHLY INTELLIGENT, VERY ARTICULATE. BUT HE WAS SORT OF ON THE EDGE ALL THE TIME.

HE COULD BE THE SWEETEST, SOFTEST, MOST CONSIDERATE MAN IN THE WORLD AND THE NASTIEST PIECE OF WORK YOU'VE EVER MET. Opposites all the time. He'd flit from one to the other. He wouldn't give a shit for anything and then he'd worry about the slightest detail.

CHARLIE: The thing about Brian is that he really was not a very strong boy.
He had this very bad asthma, and he was very weak when it came to temptations. He wasn't very pleasant really, but I think he was in a lot of pain. He was quite an unlikeable person if you got him on the wrong occasion, annoyingly so. But he was quite charming on others. He wasn't very wild - until 1964 he could handle it, then he got drinking a bit. He just drank and took lots of drugs and died.

CHARLIE: Brian wasn't helping out. I spend hours with Keith playing, that's what I do, you know. And whether we're writing a song or whether it's a Jimmy Reed number is immaterial, so long as it's working and it's fun. Brian no longer had that. We were suddenly doing sessions without him, which was unheard of.

BILL: EVERYBODY WAS BEING NASTY TO HIM. THE ENGINEERS, EVERYBODY.

Brian would play on a number and then when we played it back they wouldn't even have his fader on. He was so paranoid he'd try to play on six different instruments to try and get some effect, but it never really worked out, so he just didn't turn up, and Mick Taylor had started to come and jam with us a bit. So Brian left.

CHARLIE: **In the end it was impossible to work with him as far as things like punctuality were concerned.** He just didn't function. We were on tour in Chicago. He was really very ill and we thought 'What are we going to do?' - we carried on and the funny thing is you can do it.

BILL: Brian left by mutual consent. They didn't want him in the band any more and I think he saw that. We did a session at the Olympic studios and then Mick, Keith, and I think Charlie as well, went down to see Brian. They had a chat with him and it was agreed that he would leave the band because he wasn't contributing any more, he wasn't turning up to things.

KEITH: We went down to see him and he said, "I can't do it again. I can't start again and go on the road like that again." And we said "We understand. We'll come and see you in a couple weeks and see how you feel. Meantime, what do you want to say. Do you want to say that you've left?" And he said, "Yeah, let's do it. Let's say I've left and if I want to I can come back".

CHARLIE: Brian had left the band - he was getting a band together. I think Mitch Mitchell was going to be the drummer; he was very thrilled about it. Whether that was just talk, or whether it would have been just another 60s band I don't know, but it was a good little crowd of people he had.

MICK: He wasn't enjoying himself and it got to the stage where we had to sit down and talk about it. So we did and decided the best thing was for him to leave.

RON: I'd joined up with Ronnie Lane and Mac and Kenney after Steve Marriott left the Faces. We didn't have a vocalist at the time - Rod was too shy, lurking upstairs at the Bermondsey. Ian Stewart let us use the rehearsal place where he kept all the equipment because we didn't have any money. And then Mick rang and said "Would Ronnie be interested in joining the Stones?" and Ronnie Lane took the phone and said '"No thanks, he's quite happy where he is". I never found this out until five years later. If Mick had got through I suppose I would have been loyal and said "I don't want to let them down".

MICK: He's gotta do his own thing, man, and he hasn't said anything to us about it. 1969

MICK: **He was just gone - well, he wouldn't turn up half the time, and when he did turn up he was not in any condition to do anything. We had to baby him. It was very sad.**

CHARLIE: **He got much nicer just before he died, the last few years of his life, but I felt even sorrier for him for what we did to him then. We took his one thing away, which was being in a band. I felt.**

KEITH: **Hyde Park.** ∎ Biggest public gathering in London for over two hundred years. The last time they had a gathering that big in England, it started a people's revolt. Had to be put down with the dragoons.

RON: When they did Hyde Park I was walking around the outskirts of the park. A car pulls up and Mick and Charlie get out. They had to walk through the crowd to go and play and we just bumped into each other and they said "Hello - we'll see you, see you soon", and I said "Yeah, sooner than you think".

MICK: Brian will be at the concert. He'll be there. When we get there this afternoon...

he'll be there. 5TH JULY 1969

BILL: JUST TWO DAYS BEFORE HYDE PARK, THE OTHERS WERE AT THE STUDIO TO DO SOME OVERDUBS. I'D LEFT ABOUT ONE OR TWO IN THE MORNING AND I'D COME BACK TO THE HOTEL WITH MY GIRLFRIEND. MICK, CHARLIE AND KEITH WERE IN THE STUDIO WHEN THEY GOT THE NEWS. CHARLIE CALLED ME AND IT WAS UNBELIEVABLE. I WAS TOTALLY SHOCKED, COMPLETELY BLOWN AWAY. DIDN'T EXPECT IT AT ALL. BRIAN WASN'T A JUNKIE. I DON'T KNOW OF HIM EVER TAKING HEROIN IN ANY FORM WHATSOEVER, OR COCAINE. HE SMOKED, HE TOOK A LOT OF PILLS AND DRANK A LOT OF BOOZE - BRANDY AND STUFF LIKE THAT - AND HE USED TO MIX THEM. HE WAS ALWAYS IN THAT STATE OF HALF-AWAKE, HALF-ASLEEP, BUT I DON'T REMEMBER HIM EVER DOING ANY OF WHAT YOU'D CALL HEAVY DRUGS EVER. HE WAS JUST PILLS, PILLS, PILLS, PILLS, AND BOOZE AND TOO MUCH OF BOTH THE NEXT DAY WE MET AND WE SAID "DO WE OR DON'T WE?" AND WE DECIDED TO CARRY ON. THERE WAS TOO MUCH ORGANISATION THAT HAD GONE INTO IT, THE BIGGEST THING THAT WAS GOING TO HAPPEN IN LONDON FOR YEARS. SO MICK SAID "LET'S MAKE A DEDICATION TO BRIAN" AND THAT'S WHAT WE DID. WE ALL MET IN MY SUITE BEFORE WE WENT THERE AND MICK WAS IN TEARS. I SAID "MICK, YOU'VE GOT TO DEAL WITH IT, HE'S GONE". FROM THE DAY OF THE CONCERT IT HIT HIM AND HE GOT VERY UPSET. IT WAS A GREAT DAY. BEAUTIFUL WEATHER, BEAUTIFUL CROWD. IT LOOKED LIKE A CARPET IN FRONT OF US BECAUSE ALL YOU SAW WAS THEIR HAIR, GOING TO THE HORIZON IN EVERY DIRECTION AND UP INTO THE TREES, ALL THIS DIFFERENT MOTTLED HAIR LIKE A SHAG CARPET WITH LITTLE FACES UNDERNEATH. THEY SAY THERE WERE 250,000 PEOPLE THERE. I'D SAY IT WAS NEARER HALF A MILLION. AND THEY WERE WONDERFUL, CLEANED UP THE PARK AFTERWARDS, NO FIGHTING, NOTHING. THE ONLY PROBLEM WAS WE COULDN'T TUNE UP PROPERLY BECAUSE IT WAS A HOT SUMMER'S DAY AND IN THOSE DAYS WE DIDN'T HAVE THOSE ELECTRONIC TUNING THINGS. WE ALWAYS USED TO TUNE TO A PIANO OR A HARMONICA. THERE WAS NO PIANO, SO WE USED A HARMONICA. GOT EVERYTHING IN TUNE, LOVELY, AND WENT OUT IN THE HOT AIR, THEN ON STAGE WHERE IT WAS AIR-CONDITIONED AND WE ALL WENT OUT OF TUNE. YOU CAN HEAR IT ON THE LIVE THING, SOME OF THE TRACKS ARE REALLY OUT BUT THERE WAS NOTHING WE COULD DO. KEITH TRIED TO TUNE A BIT TO MICK TAYLOR AND I TRIED TO TUNE TO KEITH A BIT AND WE WERE ALL SLOWLY GOING IN AND OUT ALL THE TIME. THE ATMOSPHERE WAS WONDERFUL. LONDON WAS EMPTY, THEY SAY, EVERYBODY WAS OUT ON THE STREETS LISTENING, QUITE MAGICAL. BUT IT HAD THAT SAD OVERTONE OBVIOUSLY.

BILL: AFTER HYDE PARK AND BRIAN'S FUNERAL, THERE WERE THESE TWO MONTHS WHERE EVERYBODY HAD THREE OR FOUR PERSONAL THINGS HAPPEN. I'M GETTING DIVORCED; ANITA'S HAVING A BABY; MICK FLIES TO AUSTRALIA FOR NED KELLY; MARIANNE HAD A DRUG OVERDOSE OVER THERE; WE WERE BREAKING UP WITH ALLEN KLEIN. IT WAS LIKE THE JULY AND AUGUST OF 1964 WITH ALL THE MADNESS IN THE BALLROOMS.

BILL: We did this magnificent tour of America. We hadn't played for three years, really.

MICK: The real watershed was the 69 tour because it was all arenas. All of our tours before had been here, there, everywhere, in a barn one minute, a club the next, a theatre. Nobody knew whether you were coming or going, shows booked on the day we'd booked, chaotic. But the 69 tour was a tour of arenas only, with the sound hung from the ceiling. The Volkswagen van was gone forever. We had a sound system, lights of some kind and our own little carpet that went on the stage, sort of part of the little design. Clothes, stage clothes. It was the first time that I exercised and stretched and everything.

KEITH: Before, America was a real fantasy land. It was still Walt Disney and hamburger dates and when you came back in 1969 it wasn't anymore. Kids were really into what was going on in their country.

MICK: **It's more of a band now. It's definitely a different band. It's fucking incredibly hard now.**

1969

KEITH: Our sound system had usually consisted of two speakers - one of which didn't work - and all that went through there would be the vocal, and the band were supposed to provide the rest. The fact is that the audience would be louder than you. So I remember that tour mainly because it was the first time we'd had to deal with a sound system and a mixer. It had changed while we'd been off the road for three years. Suddenly you had to work with PA systems and there's an audience that's listening instead of screaming chicks. Instead of playing full blast just to try and penetrate the audiences it was back to learning how to play on stage again, so for us it was like a school again, the 69 tour.

The whole thing became much more professional, you had lights, you had your own crew. Up until then, rock'n'roll tours had been pretty ramshackle, you'd just be playing every kind of place, which is a bit disorientating for a performer. It's much easier to play the same kind of place, the same stage every night, the same configuration, it becomes like your second home.

BILL: We rehearsed in California for a couple of weeks. We were doing press, photo sessions, album cover photos, getting back into it and casual rehearsals. Rehearsal was set for seven, so Charlie would be there at seven and Keith would arrive at one in the morning and you'd rehearse till seven next morning and take the next day off. That was the start of the way the Stones worked, we never concentrated on the time. When Charlie and me toured with Clapton and the ARMS charity band, Eric used to say "OK, tomorrow morning, nine o'clock in the lobby, in the buses to go to the gig and soundcheck". So me and Charlie would wander down about five past nine, ten past. "Where is everybody?" "They ain't here yet, we're early". And they'd left at nine. We used to have to get a taxi. It was so on time we couldn't accept it, we were so used to being two hours late and still being the first ones there. It happened right till I left, me and Charlie used to be there and then you hurry up and wait..

The tour was a total success, we were going down a bomb everywhere, selling out, playing fantastic concerts. No one ever heard about that tour because it was so overshadowed by Altamont at the end. We had a great time and just to thank the American public we decided to do a Hyde Park in America and you can't do that. There are things you can do in England that you can't in America and that was one of them. It was a total mess.

BILL: TWENTY-FIVE YEARS IN THE STONES, **FIVE YEARS' WORK AND TWENTY YEARS' HANGING AROUND,** THAT WAS CHARLIE'S DEFINITION. WONDERFUL.

CHARLIE: I remember the helicopter ride to Altamont - that was like two o'clock in the afternoon. And I remember talking to a couple of guys from the Hell's Angels who were really tough guys, the real thing. Between the tent which was a sort of reception area where we were and the back of stage was a whole area full of kids bombed out, lying down, talking. Then the tent started to move a little and the Angels all had billiard cues and they went WHACK. I thought 'Well, I can't say anything because I'll get hit too'. It was like 'Blimey, that's the start of our love and peace festival'.

The stage was tiny by the time they had all these guys on there. It was awful - we couldn't play. Mick just had no room to move. And halfway through this bloody show, in the middle of something like 'Sympathy For The Devil', this motorbike comes down the middle of 500,000 people and parks right in front of the stage. The guy got really pissed off because the crowd were dancing and knocked his motorbike - and that started another fight.

CHARLIE: It was a very frightening thing really:

I just wanted to go home. It was like one of those lovely days that went all wrong.

CHARLIE: That guy pulled out a gun apparently. I remember seeing him in the crowd but I didn't see the incident. It was all very quick. Maybe one of us would have been shot. I think the Angels were far too heavy-handed, but with that guy I don't know if that was necessary. The Angels were very upset because we didn't back them - they considered they saved us, protected us, maybe saved somebody's life. Which they could well have done.

The idea was that at that period the police were considered pigs; it was a bit silly I thought, but sometimes justified. So we had local people in, people who came from that drugs, drinking, rock'n'roll crowd, so it was meant to be all right. I think they took it a bit seriously. To be fair to them, when we were checking the film of Gimme Shelter later, one of the Angels said "Well, we were doing what we were asked to do", and I suppose in a way they were. But they took authority as seriously as the coppers did. Anything that was out of line was just stomped on. And of course when you've got everyone on acid and smoking… I never took acid, ever, but I could imagine what it did.

The actual show? Jefferson Airplane played very well and the Carlos Santana Band played beautifully. That was a great band, with Micky Shrieve, but it wasn't a nice day to play music in the open air.

KEITH: It started off as a very beautiful laid-back Californian day. I remember walking through a very relaxed, nice crowd, it was love and peace. And then it all got very nasty.

The fact is that the same amount of people left as went in, because there was one killed and one born. And if you've ever seen that Gimme Shelter movie, that guy should not have been there doing what he was doing in front of those guys. Not that they should have done him in, but you are asking for trouble.

MICK: The Altamont thing was a really nasty experience but it still doesn't really sully the tour for me. That was one gig that went really wrong and it was outside the experience of that tour. We were partly to blame for not checking it out, but it was just totally disorganised. Because everyone in San Francisco was so mellow and nice and organised, you expected it was going to be all of those things, and of course it wasn't.

JIM CALLAGHAN: YOU'VE JUST GOT TO LET THEM HAVE THEIR SPACE. YOU DON'T SAY TO MICK "MICK DO THIS OR DO THAT". YOU CAN'T SAY IT TO THEM, YOU'VE GOT TO UNDERSTAND THEY'VE BEEN THROUGH MORE EXPERIENCE IN LIFE THAN MOST PEOPLE.

BILL: You'd go to Leicester and the police were lovely. They'd have a cup of tea with us before we went. In other places they were not very happy with us, but they were doing their duty. They were told to do it and were a bit difficult. But generally the police were quite friendly and helpful.

ALAN DUNN: We had John Major with us in Charlotte - he was on a lecture tour and we happened to be in the same hotel. We got talking to him in the bar, and the next day he'd decided to come. Scotland Yard thought it would be a nightmare. I heard them talking to each other - "You know it's a rock'n'roll show: they're all mad and they smash the stage". Anyway, we got them, and they came back and afterwards they said they couldn't believe how well organised it was.

TONY KING: John Major rather sweetly said "Are there any tickets left? I thought maybe they'd be sold out by now", and we sort of indicated that it wouldn't be necessary for him to line up.

JIM CALLAGHAN: We try and stop people who will intrude on their private lives, that's all we're looking for. Mick likes to roam around with his kids in the street. And people are pretty good to him. Charlie goes out - I've seen Charlie play for 100,000 people and the next day he's out shopping as if for nothing, looking round all these stores.

KEITH: **IN 1969 THERE WERE NO COPS. ALL THE COPS WERE IN VIETNAM.**

It's impossible to describe what certain parts of America, especially the West and the far West and the mid-West, were like in those years when the Vietnam war was on. There were states that were left virtually without law. People like communes, Hell's Angels, would virtually run quite significant areas. I mean, if we wanted to put on tour in the late 60s and early 70s, first off you talked to Sonny Barger, President of the Hell's Angels. Sonny's a reasonable man, you know, but if you don't talk to him you've got a fight. You didn't talk to the cops in other words, you had to talk to these outside forces.

BILL: **THE POLICE WERE SAVING OUR LIVES EVERY NIGHT. NIGHT AFTER NIGHT. WE WERE TORN TO BITS AND JUST ESCAPING.**

KEITH: **Mick figured he'd learnt enough. He was bored and thought he was now a songwriter, a producer of great stature. He had a million plans. Mick is a beautiful guitar player, amazing, but I'm still waiting.**

make his own records. I thought 'Well, this will be incredible. He's going to go from here to there'. I thought he'd be like a Pat Metheny or something. And it didn't happen. Nothing happened when he left us.

KEITH: Mick was like Eric - a lovely player, a brilliant player. But you won't have them in a band because they're not team players. They don't like being kicked up the arse and the only time you get anything good out of them is when you kick them up the arse. I'm not knocking the guy from the musical end, I'd love to work with him. But there are guys who are team players, and you say "I can live with this cat on the road", and there are other guys who might have all the credentials in the goddamn world but you can't live with the motherfucker. We're looking for a cat that wants to get into this band and stick. This is why Mick Taylor is a permanent failure to me.

RONNIE: I used to play gigs with Mick Taylor when I was with my first band, the Birds, and he was in a band called the Gods. The Birds would be supporting the Gods, or the other way round, and Mick Taylor would come up to me and say "I can't go on - will you play for me?" So I'd go on and play a half-hour set with this band the Gods and then do my set with the band. And I'd say "Mick, why didn't you go on?" He had no confidence. I had Mick Taylor's Blues Band at my club Woody's on the beach in Miami in the 80s, because I loved his playing. And sure enough he played great. I was there to support him and he came and said "Look, they're all cheering for you" and he did the same "I can't go on". I said "Come on Mick, don't give me that old shit you used to give me". But sure enough I had to go on for him again.

KEITH: I don't know the feeling. It's nothing to do with you. When it's time to go on, it's time to go on and when you get up there you either croak, puke, fall over or not.

MICK: I didn't want to go through the whole bit of auditioning guitarists, so I spoke to Mayall, a man whose judgment I respect in these matters. John just sort of grunted when I told him we'd like to see Mick, so I took it as a 'yes'. 1969

CHARLIE: It was quite difficult finding a guitar player to take Mick's place, and I don't think we ever found as musical a guitar player, but then I liked that type of playing. Ronnie is a very, very good person to have with you, and Keith prefers to play with someone like Ronnie. Ronnie's a very lovable guy. So was Mick Taylor, but he's a moodier person, a bit serious. Musically, though, Mick brought a whole other level of playing to this band. In the period he was with us I think he played beautifully. We gave him platforms to play on: he'd only do them once or twice and that was it. Usually his first go was perfect. They were really wonderful - 'Waiting On A Friend', things like that - he had a way of making a twist to them.

I never saw the reason why Mick left. Probably he was fed up or something. There were probably other reasons he left which I don't know about. But he wanted to leave to

KEITH: MICK COULD HAVE TOLD US.
WE HADN'T BEEN WORKING FOR MONTHS
BEFORE THEN. HE COULD HAVE LET US KNOW
JUST BEFORE BECAUSE HE KNEW WE HAD TO GO IN
AND START A NEW ALBUM. THE MAN'S TIMING WAS
INCREDIBLY BAD. WHY WAIT UNTIL A FEW DAYS BEFORE
WE WERE GOING TO START?

CHARLIE: I THINK WE CHOSE THE RIGHT MAN FOR THE JOB AT THAT TIME JUST AS RONNIE WAS THE RIGHT MAN FOR THE JOB LATER ON. I STILL THINK MICK IS GREAT. I HAVEN'T HEARD OR SEEN HIM PLAY IN A FEW YEARS, BUT CERTAINLY WHAT CAME OUT OF PLAYING WITH HIM ARE MUSICALLY SOME OF THE BEST THINGS WE'VE EVER DONE.

BERNARD FOWLER: AT THE BEGINNING PEOPLE WERE WALKING ON EGGSHELLS,
YOU KNOW, NOT BEING SECURE. BUT IF YOU GET THE FIRST CALL BACK,
AND THE SECOND CALL BACK, YOU KIND OF KNOW YOU'RE IN.

FOR THE MOMENT, ANYWAY.

LISA FISCHER: ON STAGE, THERE'S A SECURITY WITHOUT THERE BEING A BOREDOM. ONCE YOU FIGURE OUT WHERE YOU FIT IN AND WHAT YOUR ROLE IS, AS THE YEARS GO ON, THEY KNOW HOW TO GET YOU TO DO WHAT THEY WANT YOU TO DO.

If Mick wants to surprise me he'll do something totally out of the ORDINARY.

CHARLIE: The 1971 tour was billed as the 'Farewell Tour' because we had to leave because of tax. To make money to pay our tax we would have to make more money and then pay tax on that. We would have been in a hell of a lot of trouble: we had no money at the time and we literally lived from bit to bit. That sounds whiny - a bit Bill Wyman I call it, 'cos he always goes on about these things. **But we had no money at all.** I don't think Mick had much when you think of what he wrote up to 1969, or indeed Keith. We had a house paid for, which some would say was a lot, you've done very well, thank you very much, and that's how I used to look at it for years. But it's crazy given the amount of money this band was generating at that time. So we were moving to France. Farewell. We never called the tour that but it was filtered down to whoever was doing the press at the time.

It was a big thing to do. It was a daft thing to do, leaving England. You're English, that's where you come from.

CHARLIE: **All of us went, the whole lot, the office and everything moved over to France: it wasn't exactly known for its rock'n'roll or its vibrant young bands - very well known for Kenny Clarke and Dexter Gordon, so I loved it. We kept a place going in England but there was always Stu flitting backwards and forwards in the van. It was all very peculiar.**

BILL: WHEN WE LEFT ENGLAND AND WENT TO FRANCE AT THE END OF THE 60S WE HAD NO MONEY. FROM ONE MILLION DOLLARS YOU GOT LEFT WITH $70,000 AND YOU OWED MORE THAN THAT TO THE TAX PEOPLE SO YOU COULDN'T EARN IT SO YOU HAD TO LEAVE. THEN YOU BECOME BAD BOYS AGAIN, YOU GET ACCUSED OF BECOMING TAX EXILES TO LINE YOUR POCKETS, THE SAME OLD THING AGAIN.

117

KEITH: IT WAS NO DIFFERENT FROM ANY OTHER TOUR AT

MICK: **It was a pretty**

THE TIME BEFORE OR SINCE. IT'S THE 70S AND WE'VE GOT

wild tour. Girls,

OUR OWN PLANE FOR THE FIRST TIME, RATHER THAN

drink, you name it.

DOING IT IN THE STATION WAGON. THERE'S NOT A LOT

Rock'n'roll, even.

YOU CAN DO IN A STATION WAGON FULL OF AMPLIFIERS.

KEITH: **Since it was being filmed a lot of it was, in a way, performance - the chicks on the plane. It was done because the camera was on.**

ALAN DUNN: **During the filming of Cocksucker Blues, Robert Frank would say "I don't have any orgy scenes" or "I don't have any heavy drinking scenes" and to some degree we had to manufacture them. The famous scene on the aeroplane was very much manufactured.**

CHARLIE: **I got off the plane in 72 and said "No fucking more" because I don't actually like touring and I don't like living out of suitcases. I hate being away from home. I always do tours thinking they're the last one, and at the end of them I always leave the band. Because of what I do I can't play the drums at home so to play the drums I have to go on the road, and to go on the road I have to leave home and it's like a terribly vicious circle. And it's always been my life.**

CHARLIE: I THINK THE ROLLING STONES
ARE A GOOD ROCK'N'ROLL BAND
- WE CAN PLAY IN A CLUB
QUITE AS EASILY AS ON STAGE.
IT'S JUST ANOTHER PLACE TO PLAY.

CHARLIE: In one way stadiums are great because you can do that many people in one go and go home instead of a week-long engagement at a conference centre, which would be fine if you're not doing it for a year. When you're doing it for a year night after night it drives you up the bloody wall - it does me, anyway.

KEITH: Everywhere you go is different, especially when you're working outdoors. He doesn't let you know what He's going to be wearing that night - it could be rain, it could be snow, wind, heat, fog - all the weapons at his command. He can be aware, join in.

KEITH: **You learn that everything has to be upscaled and it's how to do it. The fact is I still use the same amp now that I would 30 years ago. It's still up there and that's the sound you're going to hear. It's how to boost it. What do you put it through to keep it sounding the same. It's all a matter of translation. At one end you're accentuating the size of something but sound-wise you're trying to minimalise it.**

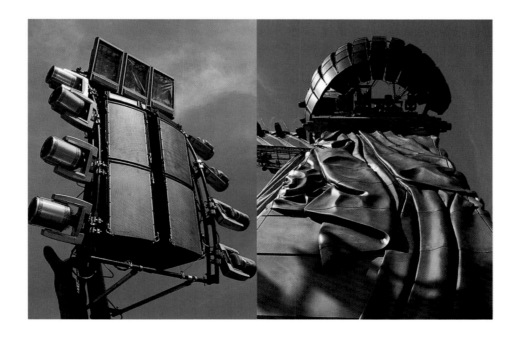

CHUCK LEAVELL:

SOMETHING THAT MARKS OUT THIS BAND IS ROUTINES, LITTLE RITUALS.

We all know the dressing set-up where Ronnie and Keith share a dressing room, that catches on. Everybody goes off in their little dressing room world, but I'll get with Mick at some point, maybe a couple of hours before the show, and make some suggestions for the set list, discuss it, finalise it, hand it over to Arnold Dunn. Arnold goes to Keith, Keith makes his decisions on his couple of numbers, and then it's printed. I go to Mick every show to warm him up, do a couple of scales and play a couple of songs, loosening him up a bit. Then the curtain goes up and there we are.

BLONDIE CHAPLIN: After the soundcheck I'll hang out, talk about the show, jam a bit on the piano, sing the keys and run in. Just kind of have a good time, it's like a vibe. They usually get around the piano and sing some old R&B songs, and clown around. You're feeling good and then you go out and do it.

CHARLIE: The only way to go on tour is to throw yourself into it. It's a very funny closed little world. The bottom line is if you don't do it properly, people who paid to see you get the rotten end of the wedge, and that's not fair. So the only way to do it, we've found, is to treat it like the army. It's strict like that.

CHARLIE: On the package tour we used to get tea and a lot of sandwiches. In pictures you can see we're always drinking tea. When we used to get to the hotel at night, there was a night porter, no room service, so you used to sit in the lounge and the porter would come with ham sandwiches. Sometimes you'd go to the kitchen and do it yourself - they used to leave it open.

ALAN DUNN: Backstage used to be the basic dressing room. You used whatever dressing rooms were available, and if you played a stadium you used whatever the teams used, a locker room. Now they're still locker rooms, they just dress them up and add a few flowers and plants.

MICHAEL COHL: On the Steel Wheels tour it was beyond anything I've seen before or since. This was a band that didn't exist, the two guys weren't talking and it was the tour that was never going to happen. We got a demand for passes that we didn't even know how to deal with. People were screaming, they were obsessed. So we created an after-show backstage pass which would get you right into the dressing room, right into the lounge, to completely empty rooms.

TONY KING: Sometimes we'll have a guest chef in and it will be sushi for the night or the local Italian restaurant will provide us with some fabulous food or if we're in the South we'll get soul food. So you never quite know what it's going to be. Everybody starves themselves till they get down here and then waits for the delivery. The billiard table is usually a local one, and the flowers and stuff. And we had Marmite delivered by Jo Wood, and so we have that backstage too. Baked beans. And HP sauce in plentiful supply for Keith - but it must be made in England. One bottle was delivered that was not made in England and it was dismissed as not being very good to go with the shepherd's pie.

RON: ON THE FIRST TOUR IT WAS ALL LUXURY TO ME. VERY SPINAL TAP:

"THESE HORS D'OEUVRES ARE THE WRONG SHAPE."

TONY KING: **There's always one shepherd's pie for the tour and one for Keith - no one must break the crust on Keith's before HE breaks the crust.**

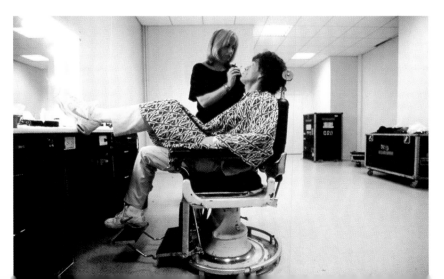

ALAN DUNN: THE IMMEDIATE TOURING PARTY AROUND THE BAND IS USUALLY ABOUT 50, PERSONAL ASSISTANTS AND SECURITY, PRESS AND FAMILY AS WELL.

BUT THE WHOLE PARTY WHEN WE'RE MOVING SHOW TO SHOW IS JUST UNDER 300.

ALAN DUNN: Even in the late 60s we were still all together in a mobile home, everybody, and we'd drive in the car park deliberately and go all through the crowd so they could see what was going on. There was no personal assistant. Ian Stewart would be looking after the back line equipment and I would be taking care of the band.

MICHAEL COHL: People are more relaxed, more professional, more confident in what they are doing, and the effectiveness of the technology has improved threefold - we can do much more with less. On Steel Wheels we had five and six on steel at one time, three stages, three sets of production. Now we've figured out how to do it with one.

CHARLIE: When you're moving a thing like this around you have to have your own people.

RON: The night Mick Taylor handed his cards in, I was at a party with Robert Stigwood and the Stones were there. I was sitting next to Mick and Taylor walked away. Mick said "He's leaving the group, he's leaving the group, I don't believe it". I said "Oh come on, he must have been kidding. He must be in a bad mood". Mick said "No he really is", then "Would you consider joining?" I said "Of course, but I can't let the Faces down". Mick said he understood but what was he going to do, so I said if he got really desperate he should ring me. A year later I was on tour in America and fell ill. The phone rang. It was Mick. He said "I'm really desperate". I said "Oh dear, all right" and I got better suddenly.

Elton John stirred it once. The Faces were playing at the Rainbow - Rod and Elton came together in the same car and Elton had told Rod "You know Woody's leaving, don't you, he's joining the Stones" and Rod was genuinely shocked. By the time I got there it had gone all round - all the boys in the band wouldn't even talk to me, a real bad vibe everywhere. I found out in between numbers on stage - "You're joining the Stones, you cunt, and you didn't even tell us". What made it worse was Mick and Keith came along to watch us, so it looked like a real pre-planned job, and it was nothing. They'd come like "OK, let's go and see Miss Stewart in her pyjamas, have a laugh". And it all got misread.

I didn't hand in my notice or anything, I decided to wait for the hand of fate to come in. I was in Geneva waiting to go to Munich. They put me in this sort of hold-over house for guitarists, waiting for these audition-type things. Somebody bought an English music paper and the headline was 'Rod Stewart Quits Faces'. That took a big weight off my shoulders, because the vibes were a little rigid between Mac and Ronnie and Rod and Kenney. Keith said "I've got a good plan. Let's not tell the press you're in the band, let's not make any announcement". Funnily enough there never was a formal statement, it just got through the grapevine.

I SUDDENLY APPEARED.

RON: THE FIRST TIME I WALKED INTO THE MUSIC MAN STUDIOS IN MUNICH I GAVE THEM A SONG IMMEDIATELY. I SAID "I'VE GOT THIS SONG THAT YOU LOT WILL LIKE" - AND CHARLIE STOPPED AND WENT "FUCKING HELL, LOOK AT HIM. HE'S BOSSING US AROUND ALREADY". IT WAS IN AN AFFECTIONATE WAY THAT HE SAID IT, BUT I KINDA GOT A CLUE THEN THAT I WAS IN. IT WAS LIKE COMING HOME TO A GANG THAT I KNEW I WOULD BE AT HOME WITH.

RON: I started off playing washboard in the Thunderbirds skiffle group. Funnily enough the last time I played washboard was on the Voodoo Lounge tour in New Orleans with the Meters. Keith and I had this party for the Stones, but we were being bothered all the time, so he said "We should get out of here, and the safest place to go is up on stage". They asked me what kind of guitar I wanted. I said "I don't want a guitar, I want a washboard". It was a real luxury job, over the shoulder. I fell straight back into it. That was great.

I saw that windswept photo of the Stones all down by the Thames, looking cold and their hair all blowing wild. But I thought "That's a proper band, I'll be in that band one day". And I always made it my mission to be in that band.

When I joined there weren't any ghosts hanging round. The sense of humour prevailed and stamped any dark clouds away. The others never really referred to Mick Taylor so I didn't feel guilty.

CHARLIE: We needed a guitar player. We recorded in Munich: I remember playing with Jimmy Page there. Then we went to Rotterdam to complete a record as well and we had a lot of guys come over there. And at that period or just after Mick and Keith were staying in the garden at Ronnie's, in what we called the shed, but was actually the old stable block down at the bottom of the garden, when Ronnie was at the Wick. He had a studio downstairs and they chucked a few demos together, and I think Ronnie kind of got playing that way.

RON: I'm still the new boy.
They still treat me like this young whipper-snapper.

CHARLIE: On Ronnie's first tour with us he went straight on and did a tour with the Faces. And I think we were in the studio before we did our tour, so he worked for a year or two years literally non-stop, with a month's break. It was quite mad for him.

Ronnie is a very diverse guy. He can play loads of instruments, he's very talented. He's very much like Brian Jones in as much as he can pick up any instrument and play it within a little while. But he's got the concentration of a gnat, so he doesn't get inside what he's doing really. He's like "Done that bit, I'm off". It's his biggest failing. It's something he likes about himself, but he can't concentrate on anything.

KEITH: I knew Ronnie's brother first: we knocked his brother's band out, ruthlessly and piranha-like destroyed the Art Wood band. We took Charlie out of there with no shame at all. Now I didn't know that Art had a younger brother - and I'm still trying to think whether I ever wanted to or not… Then, to cut a long story short, he's suddenly playing with Rod Stewart and he's a star on his own - and didn't he know it?! The way he'd dress was unbelievable. It's taken years to tone it down. But I didn't really get to meet him apart from a few hellos at hotel lobbies.

Ronnie's cutting an album down in his house. I said "Lucky sod, studio in his house". I mean, me, I'm one of the Rolling Stones and I didn't even have a tape recorder. Krissie - the first Mrs Wood - said come on over, so I went on a whim. I walk in and there's some good music going and I've got nothing much to do so I thought 'I can stay here for the night'- and stayed four, five months. I think we went on for 48 hours the first session before anybody thought of leaving. So it was "Have you got a spare room? I'll send out for a bag of new clothes". We stayed there, working and playing snooker, and worked non-stop for three or four months putting Ronnie's album together.

THAT WAS MY FIRST EXTENDED PERIOD OF WORKING WITH SOMEBODY ELSE OUTSIDE THE STONES, BECAUSE UP UNTIL THAT TIME IT WAS THE STONES OR NOTHING. PERSONALLY THERE WAS VERY LITTLE TIME AND I WASN'T INCLINED TO WORK WITH ANYBODY ELSE, BUT RONNIE CAUGHT MY FANCY.

I was in Rotterdam with no guitar player. Meanwhile we'd got Jeff Beck coming in, Harvey Mandel, Wayne Perkins. We were in the studio using a little bit of Harvey and a little bit of Wayne Perkins who played in a way very close to Mick Taylor. There was a fairly seamless stitch between him and Taylor. But it was no time to turn the Rolling Stones into an international sort of base. To me - and I think to everybody else at that time - it was really important that it still had to be all English. Somehow we got a message from Ronnie in Munich and I said to Charlie "You know who'd really fit in here is Ronnie Wood".

And Ronnie walked in and played and it was just the atmosphere between the two of us. We burn. I knew what he was capable of and what we could get out of him. At the same time I didn't want to promote him because everybody knew I'd been working with him and it could have been the kiss of death. I looked round at Charlie and Bill and Mick and it was obvious: this keeps it in the rock'n'roll game. We went on a feeling and he's still here, so we must have been right.

ALAN DUNN: In the 60s,
early 70s,
Mick was the only
one with a wardrobe.
It consisted of
one suitcase,
and I remember carrying that.

KEITH: A lot of what I'd learnt at art school came home to roost. About selling a look, an attitude, an image - like what kind of hair you wanted.

Hair's a fascinating thing.
Ask Delilah.

KEITH: I've had two showers and one bath since the start of the tour and I still smell sweeter than Jagger.

LAST NIGHT OF THE 1975 TOUR OF THE AMERICAS

MICK: On that tour I really didn't like the costumes that much. I wasn't really happy with the way I looked. I would have liked to have worn denims onstage, but you can't really dance in them. It's really easier to dance in other materials, which is a drag because I would like to dance in jeans. I never could find any street clothes that I wanted for the tour.

Sketch # 11

MICK: ACTUALLY, I THINK ROCK'N'ROLL IS ALL FRIVOLITY. IT SHOULD BE ABOUT PINK SATIN SUITS AND WHITE SOCKS.

MICK: **THAT THING WAS LIKE A MILLSTONE AROUND OUR NECKS. POLICE CHIEFS WERE WAITING FOR IT ALL OVER AMERICA. "YOU BLOW THAT BALLOON UP BIG AND I'LL THROW THE WHOLE DAMN BUNCH IN JAIL." IT WAS LIKE A DARE, YOU KNOW.**

NEW YORK

156

We rehearsed on the east coast at Montauk, at Andy Warhol's place. I had to learn, oh God, something like 260 songs. I knew their music by ear, but I'd never played it.

IN A MONTH BEFORE MY FIRST GIG I'D HAD TO LEARN 125 SONGS. I WENT ON STAGE IN BATON ROUGE ON MY BIRTHDAY, 1ST JUNE, AND I HAD 125,000 CHORDS SWIMMING IN MY HEAD.

KEITH: When Ronnie came in it was obvious to us within ten minutes that he had the heart to go tell the rest of us to fuck off. That's Ronnie. But within a matter of half an hour everybody loved him.

RON: I'LL NEVER FORGET MY REVIEW NEXT DAY IN MELODY MAKER - 'WOOD A FLOP'.

KEITH: I wouldn't say Ronnie was calming. He drove me nuts, but I was nuts anyway, so who am I to say?

RON: **We all met in the Plaza in New York. We had this flatbed truck and played early morning while all the commuters were going to work. I'll never forget playing 'Brown Sugar' with Billy Preston and all the boys, and we're going down Fifth Avenue, going past one intersection and there was Shep Gordon, Alice Cooper's manager, walking to work with his briefcase. "Hi Shep!", and he's doing a double-take.**

MICK: I think it was actually Charlie's idea. In the old days in Harlem, they used to do promotions for their gigs on the back of their trucks.

ROLLING STONES
TOUR OF THE AMERICAS '75

GUEST

ROLLING STONES
BUFFALO
JUNE 15

KEITH: **I'm always suspect of visuals. I love them but I'm also very aware that THE EYES ARE THE WHORES OF THE SENSES.**

KEITH: **The most important thing to me has always been audio. It's always been the ears. My mother's side of the family is very musical so I grew up listening to things, not looking at them. There wasn't a lot to look at when I grew up. They hadn't cleared the mess up in London from the war, and you'd turn a corner and there would be a bomb site off to the horizon.**

CHARLIE: I used to draw for a living, as a designer for an advertising agency. When I joined the Stones that's what I did.

VISUAL THINGS HAVE ALWAYS FASCINATED ME.

I went to the Opera in Kiev and they had a marvellous old-fashioned set, just three-dimensions, three curtains hanging - suddenly you're in a castle and then a garden. So I find it all interesting, especially as now I don't have to walk in with a drawing and have it criticised, which is horrible.

If I've got a bit of direction I can help it along.
I don't do the PA, I don't really know anything about it - I'm more what it looks like.

Mick is one of those people who never leaves anything to chance. Sound, costumes, lawyers, anything, he goes into it, not like me or Keith. Mick will not stand over them, but he will have numerous meetings. Mark Fisher will bring in a load of drawings and Mick will say "Oh, I think that's horrible", and I'll say "That's really great". The others aren't interested - I think Keith would say "I trust you to do that, you do it".

KEITH: **You can get quite into construction and architecture. There's the Tokyo Dome sort of model where they have double airlocks, because the air's holding the thing up. In order to do that you've got halfway to the atmosphere of Mexico City - half a mile up there's an extra atmosphere of air pressure included. And that does something to the sound...**

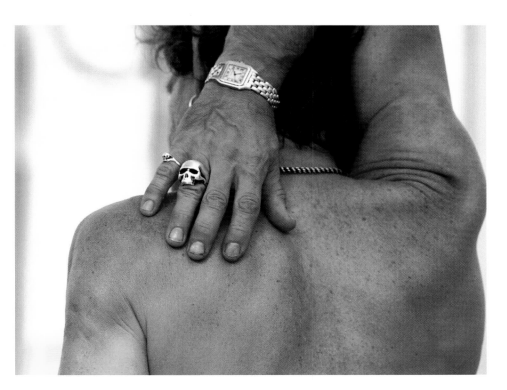

I mean music with bones, a vibration

The first time they showed me the big screen I thought 'Oh no, now we're just like little puppets, and everybody'll be watching a movie', but it didn't take me long to realise that I was wrong. It actually did help make the big places feel more intimate. Way down the stadium you're like a matchstick. You've got to work with the cameramen and you realise you can project. It just takes learning.

CHARLIE: Before a tour you're usually making a record so you're playing, which is good. And then there's that hell of a time when the phone never stops ringing, deciding what colour the backdrop is going to be, what the album cover is - Mick does most of this work, I might add - all of which gets you back into that world again. As opposed to living in the country or swanning around the world.

CHARLIE: IF YOU TURN OUT TO BE A MUSICIAN ANYTHING YOU'VE EVER HEARD COMES OUT IN WHAT YOU PLAY.

MICK: ELVIS PRESLEY WAS A BIG INFLUENCE ON EVERYBODY. HE WAS LIKE THE ARCHETYPAL ROCK STAR, STANDING THERE WITH HIS GUITAR. BUDDY HOLLY WAS VERY, VERY BIG IN ENGLAND AND WAS A GREAT ROLE MODEL FOR ANYONE THAT ASPIRED TO BEING A SINGER, SONGWRITER, GUITAR PLAYER. WE WOULD DO ALMOST EVERYTHING, SO WE'D RUN THE WHOLE GAMUT OF POP MUSIC - AND I THINK THIS IS WHAT WE STILL DO.

RON: **MICK GOES TO THE EFFORT OF LEARNING A FEW LINES IN HUNGARIAN OR SOMETHING, BECAUSE HE KNOWS FRENCH AND SPANISH AND A LITTLE BIT OF ITALIAN. THAT MAKES A BIG DIFFERENCE WHEN YOU CAN SAY THE ODD LINE TO THE MASSES IN THEIR OWN LANGUAGE.**

MICK: At some point in the show, you just lose it... You should let yourself go. I mean, have those moments when you really are quite out of your brain.

RON: With The Faces we weren't that professional. We'd go on with a rough idea of what we were playing but sometimes while we were bowing at the end we'd be going "What the fuck are we doing next, Rod?" The difference with the Stones was that they had it all planned out, they had sheets that came under your door. All these arrangements and a suggested running order. Mick would probably get together with Charlie and Keith or one or the other, and then slip it under your door, asking for any changes, anything you'd like to put in. That was very nice treatment, really, not that they would listen to any of our suggestions.

CHUCK: I started a typewritten documentation of the songs that we rehearsed, the keys they were in, the tempo we played them comfortably in, with extra notes on the arrangements. And that book has grown to be quite an encyclopedia.

MICK: WHEN WE WERE PLAYING SO MANY SHOWS IN THE 60S, I DON'T THINK WE EVER REHEARSED.

IT WAS VERY SKETCHY.

CHARLIE: On stage I watch Chuck and Keith for endings and things like that. For drive it's Keith and Darryl really. The thing with Mick is you don't see him half the time because he's gone off. On some of the stages the wings have gone right out - on one tour I never saw Mick all night. We worked it out once, he'd run about two miles a night because it was so big.

KEITH: It's usually "Oh great, it's time to go on stage. Peace and quiet". At least nobody's going to tap you on the shoulder and say "Excuse me, could you just…" That's the refuge, those two and a half hours it's all yours, buddy, and you can do what you want.

It's a matter of honour with us to deliver. And another thing is you want to cut it better than you did the night before. Sometimes you do, sometimes you don't. The aim is to top it, and if you get everybody in the right mood and at the right energy level suddenly everything elevates in you like you're not touching the ground anymore.

You're almost flying. What you see on stage is the tip of the iceberg.

MICHAEL COHL: I'd been their promoter throughout the 70s, whenever they came to Toronto. When they had that unfortunate incident in Toronto, I got the call at two in the morning. "We need $100,000 cash and we have to get Keith out of jail in the next three hours". I was scurrying around phoning every bookmaker I knew in Toronto. I thought it might stop all the touring. I figured they were never going to let this guy back into Canada, and the Americans are going to take their lead and say "That's it, and don't come back, Keith Richards".

KEITH: **They had to wake me up to formally arrest me and that took them about two hours to drag me out of bed. Rosy cheeks and he's awake.** **"You are under arrest".** **I thought 'Great', looked at the old lady and said** **"See you in about seven years, babe".**

I was down and I was out there in Toronto. And America let me in and they gave me a medical visa to clean up, and I did. That amazed me, because you don't ever expect governments to give a helping hand. This little chick from Toronto - she's totally blind - there was nothing that would stop this girl from turning up at gigs, so I'd fix her up, "Hey, give the girl a ride, man", because I had visions of her being run over and God knows what. This chick went to the judge's house in Toronto, personally, and she told him this simple story. And I think from there he figured out the way to get Canada and himself and myself out of the hole. So I was sentenced to a concert for the blind, which I gladly performed. And my blind angel came through, bless her heart.

JIM CALLAGHAN: GETTING BUSTED WAS ONE OF THE BEST THINGS THAT HAPPENED TO KEITH. 👅 THERE WAS A BLIND GIRL CALLED RITA WHO WENT TO THE JUDGE'S HOUSE AND SAID "GET HIM TO DO CONCERTS, DON'T SENTENCE HIM TO JAIL" 👅 BECAUSE KEITH WAS ALWAYS TAKING CARE OF HER, GETTING HER IN AND THINGS LIKE THAT 👅 AND KEITH WASN'T THINKING TEN YEARS DOWN THE LINE SHE'S GOING TO GO TO THIS JUDGE AND SAY "HEY, DON'T PUT HIM IN JAIL". 👅 THAT'S WHY A LOT OF IT IS HIM. KEITH HAS A GOOD HEART - AT TIMES HE LOSES HIS RAG - BUT HE DOES HAVE A GOOD HEART. 👅 SO FOR THE GOODNESS THAT HE PUT IN HE GOT IT BACK.

PRINCE RUPERT LOEWENSTEIN: The tours in America in 1975 and 1978 and in Europe in 1976 were directed by Peter Rudge. They marked the transition from the amateurish management and direction of popular musicians' stage performance in the 60s and 70s to the formation of what is now a significant part of the entertainment business. In these early years little thought was given to publicity, advertising or indeed to the production, which was by and large ad hoc and the tours summarily planned: a band got up on a stage and played to an audience with a view to becoming known and getting its new record played. 'Working a record' was the phrase, and in many cases the record companies had to supplement the income or make up the loss of these tours.

The tours of 1975, 1976 and 1978 in America, by which time the Stones played 25 concerts to three quarters of a million people were, while successful, barely profitable. Indeed the total merchandising revenue from the tour in 1978 was but a few thousand dollars.

I well remember the Los Angeles concert (where the sales of Some Girls were the highest ever for the town during the week the Stones played, for any record).

IT WAS THE FIRST OCCASION WHERE WE GOT A TASTE OF WHAT VIP HOSPITALITY ENTAILED IN A TOWN WHERE THE BROTHER-IN-LAW OF THE PHOTOGRAPHER OF THE HAIRDRESSER OF A CAMEO ACTOR IN A SMALL FILM HAS TO BE TREATED AS A VIP.

By 1981 the climate had changed and the Rolling Stones' tour was the precursor of a major trend in the entertainment business. It was the first time that a corporate sponsor was prepared to be involved and consequently where the advertising and publicity of the tour was not financed entirely out of ticket sales. This brought about the need for professionalism and for the enormously expensive productions that were necessary to satisfy the vastly increased audiences, engendered by the additional publicity.

CHARLIE: IF KEITH WASN'T VERY GOOD AT PLAYING CHUCK BERRY RIFFS, OR WHATEVER WE'RE KNOWN FOR, WE'D HAVE LASTED ABOUT TWO YEARS.

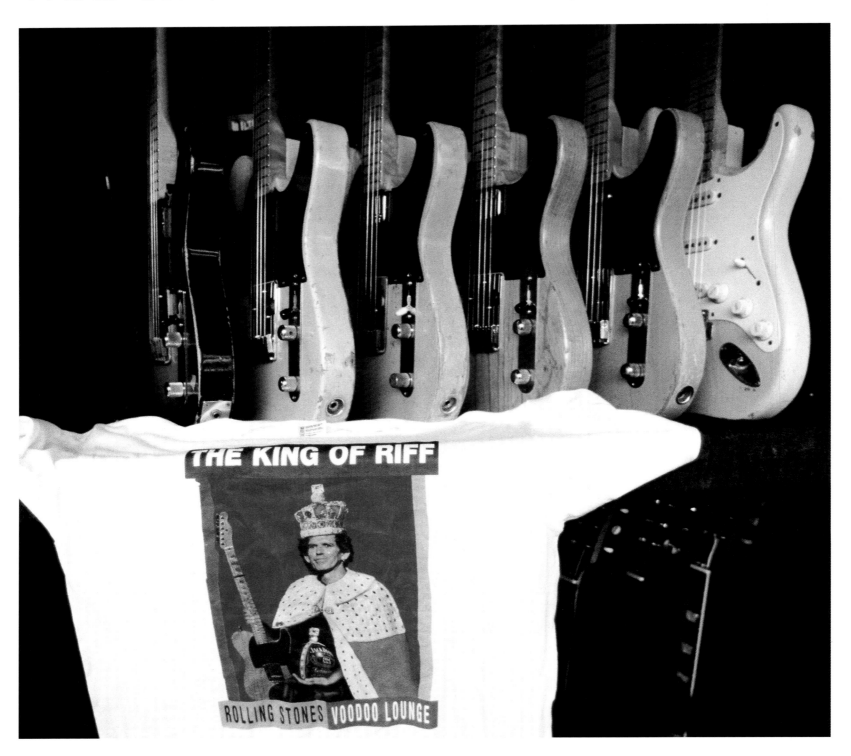

KEITH: **The shape of the guitar is very feminine. There's many times I've slept with that thing.**

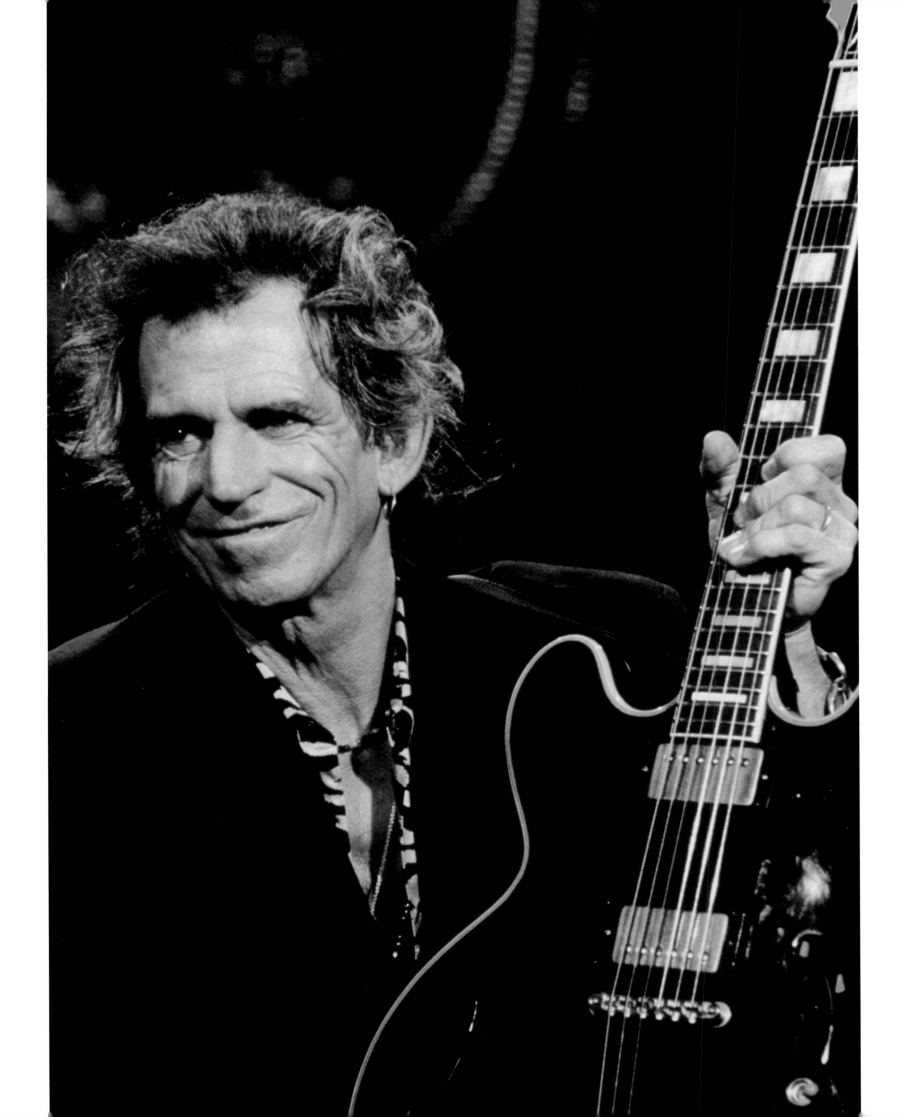

CHARLIE: KEITH'S AN ENIGMA REALLY, A VERY STRONG PERSON. SOMETIMES IT MUST HAVE BEEN A HELL OF A HEADACHE TO AGREE TO DO A TOUR, LIKE BEING A JUNKIE ON THE ROAD TO HELL.

KEITH: **Mick did his thing and I tried to keep the band together. That's always what it's been, basically. If I'm leapin' about, it's only because something's goin' drastically wrong or it's going drastically right.** 1971

DARRYL JONES: Keith is so fresh when he plays. Even when he plays the same thing a few nights in a row there is still a freshness about it. He plays in a way like the guy who just learned how to play the guitar, has learnt how to play this song well, and is now comfortable enough to try some stuff on it.

KEITH: I'VE GOT NOTHING TO HIDE. NOTHING'S A STATE SECRET WITH ME.

RON: # KEITH'S A BIT LIKE MY FATHER.

He likes to say "Where are you going?" He gets really annoyed with me if I go out in a restaurant when we're on tour. He'll say "Oh, why do you want to be seen everywhere, why don't you just order room service?" "Keith dear, I'd like to go out for once." So he'll say "Why didn't you invite me?" so we'll invite him and then he can turn it down or come. When he does come he makes a whole big deal about checking out the restaurant first, a real mafia deal. Got your seats, table, private room - he's just lovely - I just enjoy turning up.

JIM CALLAGHAN: Even now, though he's toned it down, Keith still parties to whenever. He always plays great music. I go and have a look at the albums he's playing and then go and buy them.

MICK: People that don't know you say "Well, you're on the road all the time". We're not, so when you're not on the road you can give a lot more attention to your family than someone in a nine to five job that stays late at the office. You can spend a lot of time with them when you're not on the road or when you're not in the studio. You've got maybe two months when your time is very much your own.

MICK: This is a very ruthless life if you're on your own. The only thing you've got to hang onto is family. Everybody in this band has got very strong family ties.

CHARLIE: It's very difficult to keep a marriage together when you're on the road, not so much now as earlier, because the nice thing about now is that one can dictate what you're doing. Then, you couldn't. It's harder on people around. It's a very lonely life.

CHARLIE: PERSONALLY I LOVE SHOPPING - THERE'S NOTHING NICER THAN HAVING A COUPLE OF DAYS OFF AND A LOOK ROUND THE SHOPS. I DON'T THINK MICK BUYS MUCH. WHAT HE USUALLY BUYS IS FROM SALE ROOMS WHILE WE'RE ON THE ROAD. IT'S A FASCINATION HE HAS FOR PURCHASING OBJECTS FROM THE SALE ROOMS.

The problem when you get one day off is that you're completely tired. I am lazy so it's quite an effort physically to get out.

DARRYL JONES: On a typical show day I'm usually up by about 11.30 or 12. I do a little meditation, get something to eat, and depending on where we are I might go out and do a little bit of shopping. Sometimes with Charlie.

TONY KING: Charlie stops and shops occasionally. Mick likes to play on his laptop - he's always quoting things that he's seen on the Internet.

CHARLIE: After a show I usually watch television or a video. Sometimes if I'm really up I'll put a Charlie Parker on or one of those jazz videos. I still get enormous pleasure out of watching Bud Powell or Albert Ammons.

KEITH: When I'm on the road, if I want to go out I've got to wind up five guys at least: driver, security. And what if I've wound all these people up because I'm going out and then I might change my mind. So either I go out for a walk all by myself at the weirdest times of day before anybody's about and nobody knows. Or I just say "Well I'll come back here when I'm not working".

CHARLIE: For two years we live with each other and then we never see each other - or not very often - for the next year, if not two. We've never been a great band for ringing up, although now we ring each other more now than we ever used to.

I'll often ring Ronnie to see what he's doing and he'll always tell you. It's his favourite subject.

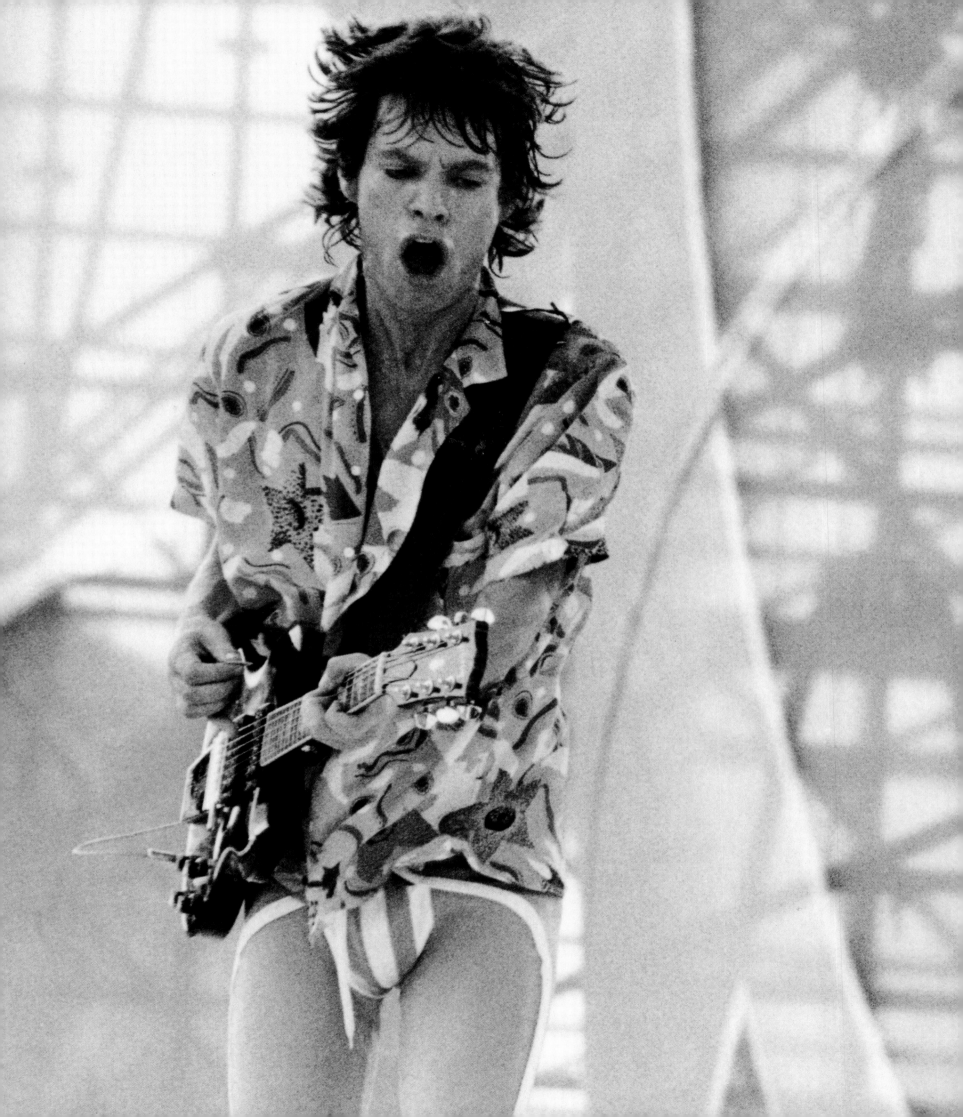

MICK: THE 1981-1982 TOUR WAS A VERY LARGE TOUR WITH A LOT OF PEOPLE. I CAN'T REMEMBER HOW MANY PEOPLE CAME TO SEE IT: ONE AND A HALF, TWO MILLION, SOMETHING LIKE THAT. IT WAS A TOUR BASED PRIMARILY ON OUTDOOR SHOWS. WE HAD TO MAKE THE STADIUM STAGE SOMETHING TO LOOK AT. WE ALSO HAD AN INDOOR STAGE DESIGNED AT THE LAST MINUTE, SO IT WAS A MIXED TOUR.

SO YOUR MOVEMENTS ARE DIFFERENT, THE BAND'S GOT TO BE DIFFERENT, THE VOLUMES ARE DIFFERENT. EVERYTHING'S DIFFERENT.

KEITH: MICK'S AND MY BATTLES ARE FASCINATING. WHEN YOU'VE KNOWN SOMEBODY THAT LONG, THERE'S SO MUCH WATER UNDER THE BRIDGE THAT IT'S ALMOST IMPOSSIBLE TO TALK ABOUT.

CHARLIE: I had a row with Mick, about attitude I suppose. With a lot of these things, when you're in a band it's a bit like having a row in the family. You know, it's over and you very rarely ever mention it again. That's what these things are like. They're like brother things. Especially with Mick and Keith.

CHUCK LEAVELL: This band is about the great songs that Mick and Keith have written through the years and the great performances that the band is known for. It should always be focused on that. The other elements of the show - staging, lighting and all - should enhance but not distract.

BILL: The first three or four years all the reporters, the writers, photographers, officials, the hotel people, the airport people, the police, everyone we came into contact with really hated us and they showed it. So it was like us against the world. It sounds a bit over the top, but it really was.

KEITH: You have to fight all these young, ageing, balding guys that are so jealous of the fact that you can do this shit and they wish you dead.

CHARLIE: When we get together something happens to people around us. When you do things on your own, you'll play wonderfully, but people just love seeing you sitting there playing 'Brown Sugar' with Keith on guitar. If it's somebody else it's not going to be the same. I don't know what it is, unless it's something we've created and hung onto - it might be an illusion.

CHARLIE: When I first met Mick and Keith, one was middle-class and at university - there's nothing wrong with either of those things, in fact they're very commendable - and the other was more like me and never went to work. Keith's never changed what he's like, he's still the same as he ever was. I suppose Mick is too, really. Mick's very clever at picking up on things and learning. They're as close now as they were when they were kids. Or perhaps they were as different in their ways when they were 19 as when they were older. The only thing that brought us all together was the fact that we were trying to play in a band.

MICHAEL COHL: WHEN THEY HIT THOSE STAGE STAIRS WHATEVER ELSE HAS HAPPENED DOESN'T EXIST. EVEN WHEN THEY'RE NOT GETTING ALONG THEY GET ON STAGE AND THE MAGIC CLICKS.

KEITH: **It's not Bach or Beethoven. It's not like you've got to play it this way note for note. You get out there, you *know* the feeling. The whole thing is about improvisation. Here comes the blues again, and it keeps coming...**

CHARLIE: I don't move. I hate moving. The others did try and have me on a stall that went up. I used to hate the sort of risers Ringo went on. They always wobble. So I have a foot-high one, always this set size, on a Persian rug. That's it. That's me. All the bit round it is all frills, but the frills are very important to Mick because he has to work them so much, and Keith is very good at it now.

KEITH: CHARLIE SOMEHOW IS NEVER SHOW BUSINESS. IN THE LIST OF THE BEST ROCK'N'ROLL DRUMMERS OF ALL TIME, HIS NAME'S GONNA BE AT THE TOP OF THE LIST, BUT CHARLIE CRINGES FROM THE WHOLE IDEA OF BEING A SHOWMAN.

CHARLIE: I missed one show because I got the wrong date. The others all say no, I didn't, I stayed on holiday an extra day, but I didn't. Micky Waller played the drums, really well - much to my chagrin. I'd been staying in Ibiza and came back on the 19th and we'd had a gig on the 18th. I remember distinctly walking in and someone saying 'Where were you?" I said "I was in Gibraltar last night". We'd been in Catford or somewhere and everyone was raving about Micky.

I don't really hit very hard. If you play them long, they get really big. That's how blues drummers get that great sound, by playing with the longer bit of the stick. When you hit that, you don't really have to hit it that hard - just constantly, and that's a bit of a sod, especially when it's cold and outdoors.

Mick's the one who's performing the songs, the way I see it. All I do is help them do this. That's the function of a good drummer.

It's absolutely true. Drummers must swing. If they don't, nothing is ever going to happen with the music. And I'm talking about the most avant-garde type of player - Tony Williams: you'd dance to him - and that is a great drummer. Or Earl Palmer - on any of Little Richard's stuff - that to me is a fantastic drummer.

DARRYL JONES: I play with drummers, first and foremost, because I feel we're the engine, the locomotion of the band. I'm sure a lot of the other guys who auditioned looked at Keith and Mick in front of them and in a way played to them. I just turned around and looked at Charlie and listened very carefully to *him*.

BILL: If the drummer shows off he just gets in the way of everybody else. So Charlie was perfect. He had that jazz feel, and he'd played with Alexis Korner, and we formed a good foundation very quickly for the rest of them.

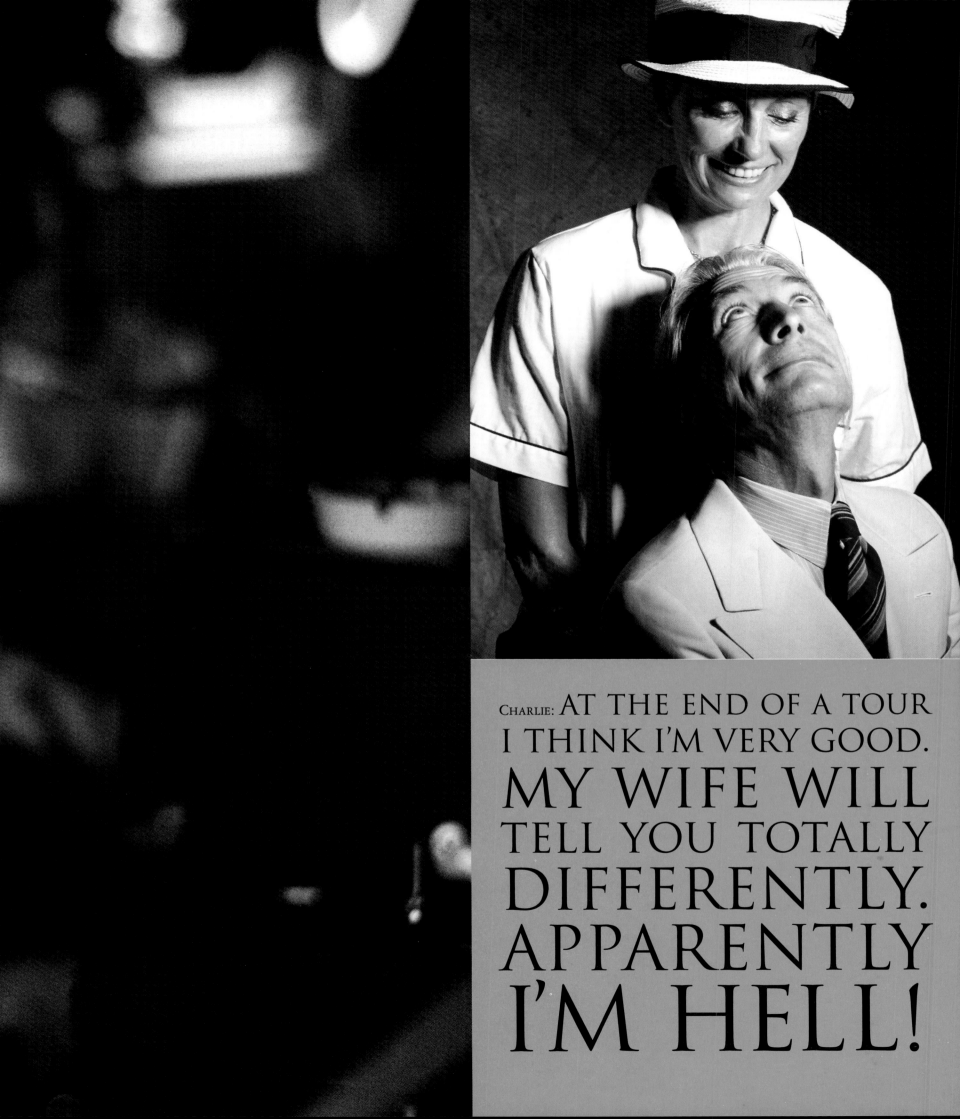

CHARLIE: AT THE END OF A TOUR I THINK I'M VERY GOOD. MY WIFE WILL TELL YOU TOTALLY DIFFERENTLY. APPARENTLY I'M HELL!

MICK: **You seem to be split** in various parts.

And there's this other part of you, which is just your body doing things that it isn't really commanded to do, which I found is the dangerous part.

There's part of you which is saying to you

"OK, DON'T FORGET THIS, DON'T FORGET THAT".

MICK: I was feeling very stultified within the Rolling Stones and I felt I had to go and work with some other people to get a bit revitalised. I think it worked although it created a tremendous ruckus within the Rolling Stones, which was totally unnecessary really. I think everyone made much too much of a fuss about it. Everyone should have been a bit more indulgent.

KEITH: Hell, we needed a break. Mick needed to play on his own out there and see what it's like, to see if he thought he could live without us, and I had to find out and do it myself too. We both grew up a lot doing and finding out certain realisms. It's easy to go a little crazy inside the Rolling Stones bubble if that's all you do.

MICK: The difficulty in growing up, I think, is that you start with this gang of people, and, as anyone knows who's been in a gang, the gang simply can't last forever. It's very childish to think you can remain in this gang all the time.

KEITH: **I guess everybody had a sort of learning experience.** Charlie put his jazz band together - and he found out all about running a bunch of blokes around the world, whereas with the Stones it would never have entered Charlie's mind to be involved with that.

And he had to deal with the day-to-day business of a bunch of guys in a foreign country going "Ooh, I can't find any egg and chips" or "I've lost my money".

And I learned a lot more. I had a lot more sympathy and understanding for Mick, for what it's like to be the front man.

KEITH: STU WAS THE ONE WHO ORGANISED THE STONES. IN A WAY IT'S STILL HIS BAND.

I probably speak to Stu just as much now as I did before he died. It's the nod of approval, passing things through what you imagine Ian Stewart's critical judgment would be. Knowing Stu, nine-tenths of the time it's going to be "all fucking rubbish", which is a damn hard criteria. Because you've got to get to that other one-tenth to get him to smile.

RON: STU WAS, YOU KNOW, STU WAS STU. IF YOU GOT A PHONE CALL FROM HIM YOU KNEW IT WAS HAPPENING. WHEN HE DIED, WE WERE ALL AT THE FUNERAL AND CHARLIE SAID TO ME "WHO'S GOING TO BOSS US AROUND NOW?" - IT WAS A REAL TEAR-JERKER.

BILL: Stu. Stu did everything. He booked the hotels if we had to stay overnight. He loaded the vans, he unloaded them, set the gear up, looked after us and then played piano as well if we wanted him to.

KEITH: His love for the band, his thing of keeping it together was beyond any monetary thing, beyond any ego - he just heard this band and said "All right, make it happen". And he did it almost single-handedly. It was basically Stu's will - we had plenty of our own, but we wouldn't have been able to pull it together.

BILL: Stu worked himself to the bone. We'd be driving home after dropping the guys off at two in the morning or something and I'd wake up and find us parked in some layby. Stu'd be asleep. I'd say "Stu, where are we?" - "I've got to get some sleep." "It's quarter to six, where are we?" - and then I'd find where we were and off we'd go again. I'd drop off to sleep and we'd be parked again. He was so asleep he'd be all over London in all the wrong directions, and we'd finally get to my place at about quarter to eight. I think that part of his early death was caused by all that.

CHARLIE: Stu was sober, but he was very eccentric. The first time I met him he had a pair of shorts on, which was horrendous to me. And he played this music that I never really knew, boogie woogie stuff. I knew Meade Lux Lewis but that was it.

MICK: *Stu was always different from us.* He was part of the band musically, but he wasn't in some ways part because he had a real job, a real house. And he played a piano rather than an electric instrument. And although he liked blues he wasn't really into all this stuff that we used to play, all the rock'n'roll music. *He was very different.*

CHARLIE: Stu was a member of the band during the club period, he was the piano player. And then when we were at the Station Hotel in Richmond and Andrew got involved, Stu was deemed not good-looking enough and certainly not hip enough to look at. He never changed that look he had. He wore those golf shirts - and the week he died he looked exactly like the first time I saw him. He loved playing and he liked the band but he left his job and did the driving and setting up the amps and that. It must have been awful for him really. At the time I didn't really think about it to be honest. We were very cruel really. Even when Ian McLagan or Chuck Leavell used to play with us Stu would still play the piano but they'd hide him under the footlights or something. In the end he became a feature. Keith loved him and certainly loved playing with him. Nobody quite played with that lope Stu had. People like George Green used to rave about Stu: he had a very crude way of playing but it was dead right actually. But Stu would never change - that was typical of him. If you were playing a ballad or something he'd never change that dum de dum de dum. And if he didn't like it, he'd just stop playing until it came back.

BOBBY KEYS: The first time I was really aware of the Stones was the beginning of the British invasion, when I heard a track they had recorded - 'Not Fade Away' - written by Buddy Holly. I thought "These English bastards, how blasphemous, how dare they?" And then I first ran into them in San Antonio, Texas at the Dick Clark Teenage World Fair. I was playing with Bobby Vee, a real teenage heart-throb. We were all staying in the same hotel, and I remember thinking

"God, I've never seen people with such white skin in all my life".

And they had really rather unusual bathing suits. These guys said "Oh, we ought to change clothes", and I ended up wearing a pair of Bermuda shorts and cowboy boots on stage, which was completely noticeable: everyone else was in mohair suits, high-collared shirts and silk ties. And the boss didn't like that at all.

CHARLIE: He was with Bobby Vee or somebody, who was on the bill with us, and they actually had Bermuda shorts on. We had trousers on, sort of the Soho type. We were walking around in this boiling hot weather, completely out of place.

BOBBY KEYS: I did 'Live With Me' on Let It Bleed when they were in the Electric Studios in LA - I just happened to be in the studio at the same time. Then Jim Price and I had been flown over to England by Robert Stigwood to be part of the Derek and the Dominos band. And somewhere between the time we left Los Angeles and went into Heathrow they decided they didn't want to use Stigwood - Eric felt a bit guilty about us coming all the way so he hooked us up with George Harrison who was doing All Things Must Pass. We were staying up at George's house in Henley and I just ran into Mick one night at a club in London. He said "We're out here, man, why don't you drop by, bring your horn with you?", so I did. The first thing I did was a song called 'Can You Hear Me Knocking'. That worked out OK. And then I did a solo on 'Brown Sugar' and that worked out OK too. After the recording of Sticky Fingers, Jim Price and I had weaseled our way into a gig. We'd woven our way into the fabric and we thought 'Thank God'. The crowds weren't as large because the venues weren't as large, but they were in heaven. These guys had some real rocking fans, you know. People were going to burn the place down.

CHARLIE: WE MET BOBBY KEYS IN SAN ANTONIO ON THE FIRST TOUR OF AMERICA, THAT'S HOW LONG WE'VE KNOWN HIM.

BOBBY KEYS: # NOW WE'VE GOT GOLF BALLS WITH TONGUES ON THEM. NOT LIKE THE 70S WHEN WE HAD BALLS WITH TONGUES ON THEM: WE DIDN'T KNOW WHOSE TONGUES THEY WERE.

WE HAVE GOT LOGOS ON THE HEAD COVERS GOING OVER OUR GOLF CLUBS... AND WE HAVE THE VOODOO LOUNGE GOLF SHIRT: ON THE BACK IT LISTS EVERY COURSE WE PLAYED AND THE DATE, AND IT'S IMPRESSIVE AS HELL... GLENEAGLES, TROON. WE STAYED AT GLENEAGLES IN 1970. IAN STEWART USED TO BOOK US INTO THESE PLACES. WE'D END UP STAYING AT THESE GOLFING RESORTS, AND OF COURSE AT THAT TIME GOLF WAS NOT ON MY MIND OR ANYBODY ELSE'S EXCEPT IAN STEWART'S.

I think of Stu often. I was out on a golf course with Alan Dunn and I said "Can you imagine now if Ian Stewart is looking down upon us from up above - what he would think of this situation: Bobby Keys out here trying to play golf…" He'd say

"Oh God, what a load of bollocks".

MICHAEL COHL: THIS WAS A BAND THAT DIDN'T EXIST, TWO GUYS WHO WEREN'T TALKING, AND THE TOUR THAT WAS NEVER GOING TO HAPPEN. SO WHEN IT DID, IT WAS BEYOND ANYTHING I'VE EVER SEEN BEFORE OR SINCE.

KEITH: The miracle about that gap in touring was that it wasn't the end of the world for us. To come back and get it together again for Steel Wheels for me was like "Get back together and do something interesting, or it won't get back together".

MICK: We had a meeting to plan the tour, and as far as I was concerned, it was very easy. At the time, everyone was asking "Wow, what was it like? What happened? How did it all work?" It was a non-event. What could have been a lot of name-calling, wasn't. I think everyone just decided we'd done all that. Of course, we had to work out what the modus vivendi was for everybody, because we were planning a very different kind of tour. We had to invent new rules. It was bigger business, more efficient than previous tours, than the 70s drug tours. We were all gonna be on time at the shows. Every one realised they had to pull their weight, and they were all up for doing it.

RON: I thought that after the seven year lay-off time from touring and the recent re-amalgamation of Mick and Keith, I just sensed the vibe like, they know I've got a lot of ideas, but they wanted to get their Glimmer Twins thing back together - and I respected that.

Michael Cohl: **3,400,000 people in 59 shows.**
Nothing's ever come close.
Unbelievable.

TONY KING: I think Steel Wheels upped the ante for me. I don't think anyone had ever done it in quite such a way. It seemed to me to be a time when the Rolling Stones took a slightly different direction and maximised their earning potential.

CHUCK LEAVELL: There was an enormous jump from 1982 with the staging and lighting and so on. And also in the length of time that the band rehearsed prior to the tour: a good two months, maybe even more. There was a lot more care and attention given to the songs that we might play, and that carried on through Voodoo Lounge and the Bridges To Babylon tour.

ROLLING STONES STEEL WHEELS

· Philadelphia
· Toronto · Pittsburgh
East Troy · Cincinnati · Raleigh
· St. Louis · Louisville · Syracuse · Washington
· Cleveland · Boston · Birmingham · Ames · Denver
Los Angeles · New York City · Vancouver · Oakland
Houston · Dallas · New Orleans · Miami · Tampa · Atlanta
Jacksonville · Minneapolis · Indianapolis · Detroit · Montreal

NORTH AMERICAN TOUR 1989

ROLLING STONES

URBAN JUNGLE

Tour Dates

JULY 4 · LONDON WEMBLEY STADIUM
JULY 6 · LONDON WEMBLEY STADIUM
JULY 7 · LONDON WEMBLEY STADIUM
JULY 9 · GLASGOW, HAMPDEN PARK
JULY 11 · CARDIFF ARMS PARK
JULY 13 · LONDON, WEMBLEY STADIUM
JULY 14 · LONDON WEMBLEY STADIUM
JULY 18 · NEWCASTLE

JULY 20 · MANCHESTER, MAINE
JULY 21 · MANCHESTER, MAINE
JULY 22 · EXCLUSIVE BROADCAS
ON SKY TELEVISION 8F
JULY 28 · EXCLUSIVE BROADCAS
ON SKY TELEVISION 5F

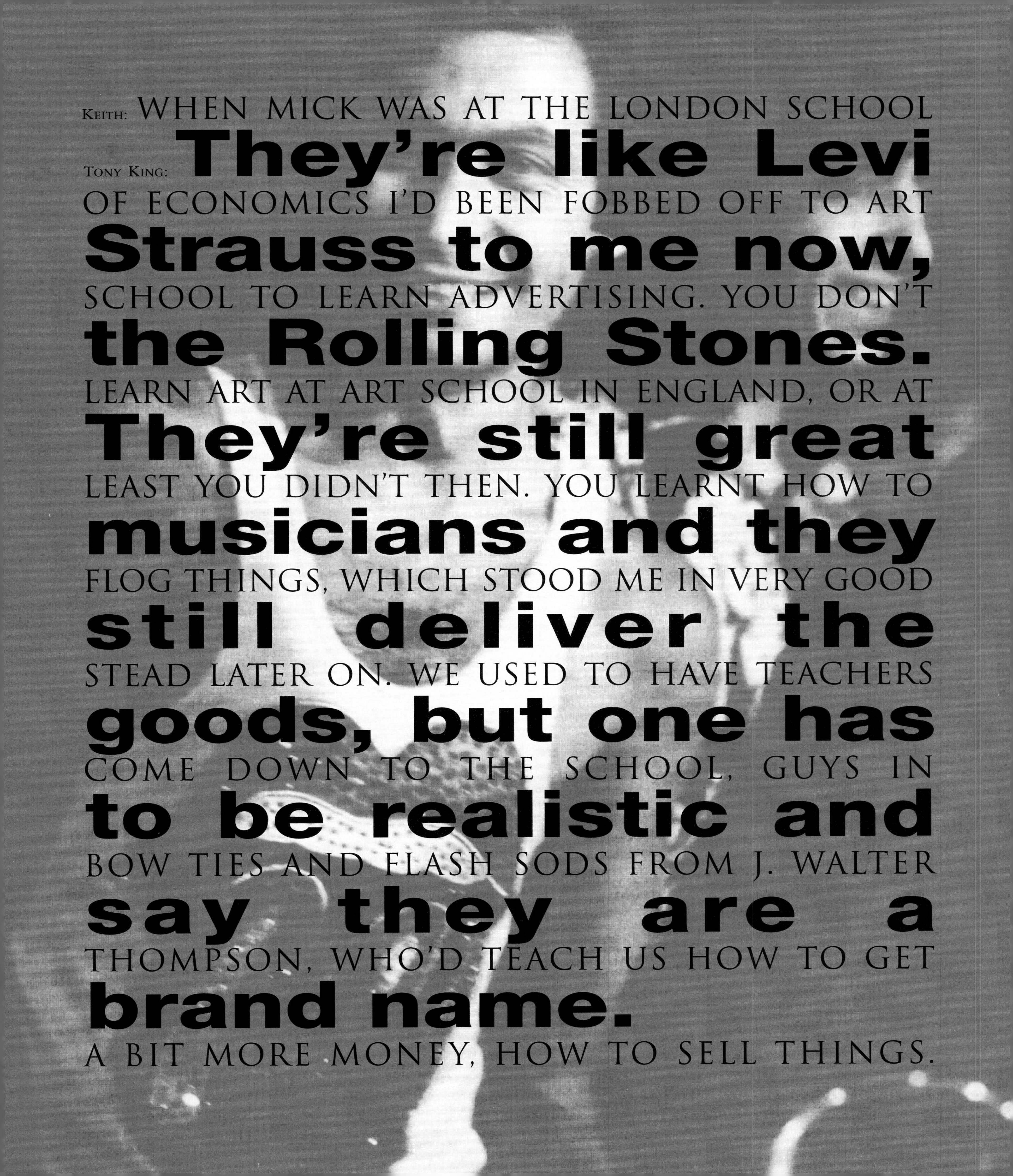

KEITH: WHEN MICK WAS AT THE LONDON SCHOOL

TONY KING: **They're like Levi**

OF ECONOMICS I'D BEEN FOBBED OFF TO ART

Strauss to me now,

SCHOOL TO LEARN ADVERTISING. YOU DON'T

the Rolling Stones.

LEARN ART AT ART SCHOOL IN ENGLAND, OR AT

They're still great

LEAST YOU DIDN'T THEN. YOU LEARNT HOW TO

musicians and they

FLOG THINGS, WHICH STOOD ME IN VERY GOOD

still deliver the

STEAD LATER ON. WE USED TO HAVE TEACHERS

goods, but one has

COME DOWN TO THE SCHOOL, GUYS IN

to be realistic and

BOW TIES AND FLASH SODS FROM J. WALTER

say they are a

THOMPSON, WHO'D TEACH US HOW TO GET

brand name.

A BIT MORE MONEY, HOW TO SELL THINGS.

RON: IT WAS A SHAME WHEN BILL LEFT, AN ORIGINAL MEMBER. BUT I COULD UNDERSTAND HE WAS 2000 YEARS OLD, HE'D HAD ENOUGH OF TOURING. BUT WE WEREN'T GOING TO STOP JUST BECAUSE BILL LEFT. LIFE GOES ON.

RON: We had great fun auditioning bass players. I think we did nineteen in one day. There were lots of my friends I didn't even put in for the job because I didn't want to barge around. It was difficult because all the bass players were incredible. I have a book of every day of auditions, who they were, my comments on them. Mick kept notes. All of us, maybe mental notes. But I wrote them down and Mick did and I think Keith would come up and put things on my sheet like "This guy stinks" or "He was great".

The first songs would be, say, 'Brown Sugar' and 'Miss You' and then a blues jam to see how solid they were or how they kept with Charlie. It's very hard for these talented people, for us to treat them like "Next!", but they all understood we had a big job on our hands.

KEITH: Bill was totally rock'n'roll but when he started to play we realised there was no fucking difference at all. We called it an R&B band because Charlie wouldn't play in a rock'n'roll band. Bill Wyman swung with Charlie and there was no doubt about it, but looking at the two it was the most unlikely chemistry. The difference between North and South London was enormous.

RON: WHEN BILL WAS WITH THE GROUP, BEFORE HE GOT THE NOTION NEVER TO GET ON AN AIRPLANE AGAIN, HE WAS INCREDIBLY SUPPORTIVE TO ME. I WOULD SORT OF SAY "BILL, HELP ME" AND HE USED TO STEP IN AND JUST THANK ME IN FRONT OF THE REST OF THEM, AND SAY "YOU'VE DONE SO MUCH GOOD BLAH BLAH BLAH". HE DIDN'T CARE ABOUT THE CONSEQUENCES. CHARLIE WAS VERY SUPPORTIVE TOO. THEY WERE THE ONES WHO GOT ME ON AN EQUAL WAGE.

DARRYL JONES: The reason I even pursued working with these guys is that I thought what I do as a bassist could work with what they do. I hold solid ground. That's what I've done with everyone that I've ever worked with. So when I auditioned for them I remember leaving the audition thinking to myself 'That felt good, and if it felt as good to them as it did to me then I will hear from them again'. And I guess it did.

CHARLIE: FOR YEARS I NEVER TALKED TO THE PRESS.
SOMEBODY ASKED ME WHY I DIDN'T AND
I SAID "WELL, I DON'T REALLY FEEL LIKE
TALKING. I DON'T LIKE IT". I STILL DON'T.
I TRUST THE OTHERS TO SAY WHATEVER
THEY SAY ON MY BEHALF.
THEY NEVER SAY THINGS I DISAGREE WITH.
I'M NOT VERY SOCIABLE.
I'D RATHER BE SITTING LISTENING TO THE RADIO.

MICK: Andrew pitched it so that we were very much the antithesis of the Beatles, but the reality of the Beatles was they were just as cynical as us, but they'd been pitched as clean-scrubbed, and they'd got the suits and so on. We were billed as this black version of them - and of course, when you look at the pictures you can see how clean and sweet we really were.

KEITH: At the beginning of all this, in the early 60s, nobody took the music as seriously. It was image that counted. They were very hip to image and how to manipulate the press and dream up a few headlines. A lot of PR went into it. Without consciously doing it, it was just like "What mood do we make today - come on, Andrew, let's dream up a gig, some gag".

Rome

TOUR

LAM...
PLAS...

...VER...
...AGENT...

...RPLE...
...OLA

...AMINA...
VIP

...GREEN...
— VERDE...

GLI ACCESS...

...ACCESS

...LI ACCESSI...
...NG ROOM
...ERINO

<u>NO</u> STAGE ACCESS
NO PALCO

STICK ON   **WORKING PERSONN...**
...TTACCATO   PERSONALE DEL LAVO...
ALL ACCESS

TUTTI GLI ACCESSI
...OM

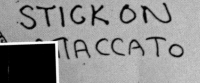

Purple V·10

PURPLE
Guest PASS
PASS PER OS

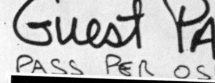

ON **VIP PASS**

VIP PASS

MUST HAVE TICKET

DEVONO AVERE IL BIG

M

AFTER SHOW PASS

PASS PER DOPO SHOW

T

NO AVERE IL

STAGE AF

STAGE SOLO

MINATE

ALL ACCE

WORKING
PERSONNEL

WORKING
PERSONNEL
Nº 010

KEITH: THE BAND IS GETTING BETTER AND BETTER.
THE GUYS ARE KNOCKING ME OUT, YOU KNOW,
AND THAT MAKES ME HAPPY
AND IF I'M HAPPY IT KEEPS EVERYBODY ELSE HAPPY
BECAUSE WHEN I'M UNHAPPY, FORGET ABOUT IT. 1995

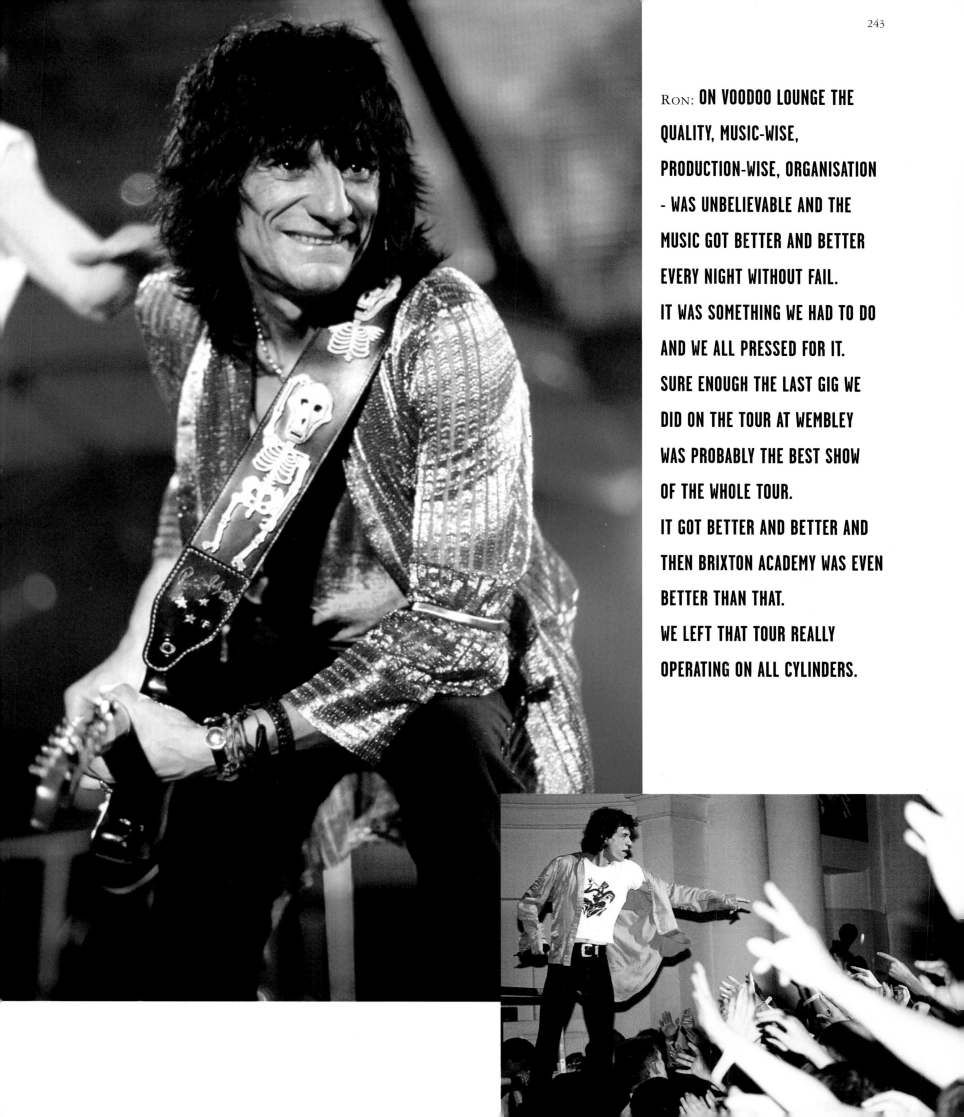

RON: **ON VOODOO LOUNGE THE QUALITY, MUSIC-WISE, PRODUCTION-WISE, ORGANISATION - WAS UNBELIEVABLE AND THE MUSIC GOT BETTER AND BETTER EVERY NIGHT WITHOUT FAIL. IT WAS SOMETHING WE HAD TO DO AND WE ALL PRESSED FOR IT. SURE ENOUGH THE LAST GIG WE DID ON THE TOUR AT WEMBLEY WAS PROBABLY THE BEST SHOW OF THE WHOLE TOUR. IT GOT BETTER AND BETTER AND THEN BRIXTON ACADEMY WAS EVEN BETTER THAN THAT. WE LEFT THAT TOUR REALLY OPERATING ON ALL CYLINDERS.**

RON: THE GREAT THING WAS MICK AND KEITH WERE GETTING ALONG SO MUCH BETTER. WHENEVER THEY THOUGHT A LITTLE **FEUD** WAS COMING UP,

THEY WOULD SAY "OH, I GUESS WE'D BETTER DO
'SWEETHEARTS TOGETHER' TO COOL THINGS DOWN".
THEY DO NICE **HARMONY**.

TONY KING: **When they walk on stage they're not just musicians, they carry a lot of history with them. You see their talent, but you are also watching that reputation and they know it. They work hard to live up to it. They don't slack, they don't coast, they don't pretend they're big enough so they don't have to do much. They go out and give it 110%.**

CHARLIE: I don't think we could have done it without the perks. The days when you sat at Mrs Cleethorpes' place, had bed and breakfast and went out - that's when you're young. Doing it when you're 50 or whatever's a bit much. It's much easier now. I always say I could ring the office and say "Can somebody carry me into the gig?" I could be carried in and woken up when I've got there. So long as you're well for two and a half hours, which would just about get you through the show, that's fine.

MICHAEL COHL: From my perspective they seem to be at least as healthy as they were, but having a much better time.

JIM CALLAGHAN: Mick wants to be around when he's 90 so he really looks after himself. People don't realise that this man is dedicated. To go on stage when you're 54 and do things you might do when you're 21, there must be some effect. But he goes on there and he does it. He's fit, but there's so many chances to say "Oh, fuck this, I'm going out to bang one up" but he doesn't. He's there for his art and his craft.

KEITH: The energy's always been there, but I think that we can now hear what we're doing better. There's less confusion on stage - that's to do with sound systems and monitoring. If the band can hear itself you can focus the energy, the band's confident that what they're playing and their idea of what they should be sounding like is going on out there. So I wouldn't say that the actual amount of energy is any more or less but it's all coming down one tube at you now. It's not dispersed.

BLONDIE CHAPLIN: They love music so much. That energy comes from being addicted to music, that's the central passion. They have to want to dig playing to continue and continue and continue.

Keith: I DON'T DO ANYTHING TO PREPARE FOR A TOUR. MAYBE I DON'T HAVE TO THINK ABOUT IT ANY MORE BECAUSE I'VE BEEN DOING IT ALL OF MY WORKING LIFE. FOR ME IT DOESN'T START UNTIL I'VE GOT

CHARLIE ON THE DRUM STOOL,

RONNIE THERE,

MICK THERE,

AND I FIND OUT WHERE EVERYBODY'S AT. THAT'S THE BEGINNING OF THE PREPARATION. IT'S LIKE I DON'T HAVE TO WORK OUT, I PLAY WITH THE STONES. YOU DO A TWO AND A HALF HOUR SHOW A FEW TIMES A WEEK AND YOU DON'T HAVE TO WORRY ABOUT WORKING OUT, AT LEAST FOR ME.

If you want any more exercise, go fuck, you know.

CHARLIE: The only thing I worry about when I do the first show is whether my hands will hold up. And you hope you've rehearsed enough. Not necessarily in terms of knowing how the songs go, but physically. That's why, although they tend to be very boring - and Bill used to hate them - long rehearsals are good because they're like practice time. You can't practise in your room. I mean, you can sit on the bed with some sticks, but nothing helps you when you're physically playing with a band. If you stop the whole bloody thing stops.

KEITH: These tours develop their own strains of bacteria and bugs. They make their own diseases. There's always somebody under the weather or somebody's broken something. There are constant repairs going on all the time.

KEITH: Steel Wheels wasn't a bad getting back together and Voodoo Lounge wasn't a bad follow-on through. Babylon fuelled the band. One way or another we needed to take some chances again and go into some different areas.

CHUCK LEAVELL: The music has always come first and foremost, although there have been times when I think we've run a bit of a danger of having too much fanfare, too many bells and whistles. On Babylon it was pared down a bit - and that was good.

KEITH: I think Babylon was the first tour where the sound system was not a central tower which cut off your vision. It blocked off your perception of where you were playing because there were lights on it and so you thought that was the end of the stadium. For the first time we could actually see how big the joint was: "Wow, this place is big, I didn't realise". Before you couldn't see half the audience. You could feel them, maybe...

CHARLIE: We started the tour in Chicago without a bridge and when we finally got the moving thing, I said to Mick "I just realised people must have thought we're mad". We'd got this title and no bridge. A bit like Concorde without the aeroplane.

JIM CALLAGHAN: They're there for their art and their craft and you have to admire them for that. Like the bridge: I'm going "Who needs a fucking bridge, we've got a ramp" and it costs you about $100 to put up a ramp. No, they want a bridge that costs a million and a quarter for one minute's feel. And that's it. That's what they want because they add their little bit to it.

KEITH: **The closer and lower you get to bury yourself into the audience, the harder it gets, but the better it gets. And that's an interesting thing to learn because when you're playing at one end of a football stadium all the time, you've always got the people down the other end.**

We're trying to bridge that gap.

MICK: THE BIG CHALLENGE WHEN YOU'RE PLAYING THESE VERY BIG STADIUM SHOWS IS TO REALLY ENTERTAIN PEOPLE, BECAUSE THAT'S WHAT MAKES THOSE BIG SHOWS WORK. 👅 YOU WANT TO HAVE GREAT SOUND 👅 YOU WANT TO HAVE A REALLY GOOD PERFORMANCE FROM THE BAND 👅 YOU WANT TO HAVE SOME THINGS THAT PEOPLE CAN TAKE HOME IN THEIR HEADS GOOD SPECTACULAR MOMENTS 👅 AND YOU WANT TO CREATE DIFFERENT MOODS. SO YOU TRY AND BALANCE ALL THOSE THINGS. 👅 IT'S LIKE IN A 19TH CENTURY OPERA WHERE THEY HAD VERY, VERY BIG EFFECTS AND IT DROVE PEOPLE CRAZY, SO YOU WANT TO BALANCE THE SONGS WITH THIS BIG SPECTACULAR SHOW **THIS IS THE CHALLENGE.**

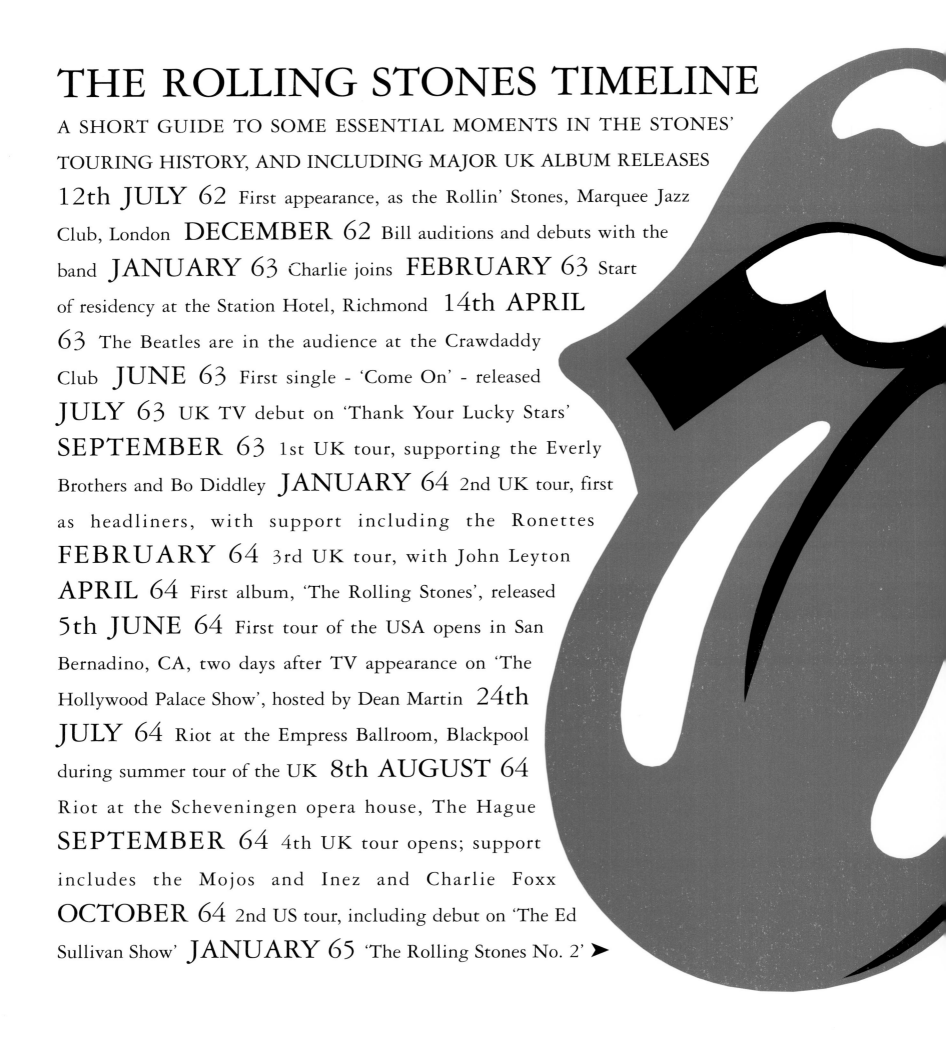

THE ROLLING STONES TIMELINE

A SHORT GUIDE TO SOME ESSENTIAL MOMENTS IN THE STONES' TOURING HISTORY, AND INCLUDING MAJOR UK ALBUM RELEASES **12th JULY 62** First appearance, as the Rollin' Stones, Marquee Jazz Club, London **DECEMBER 62** Bill auditions and debuts with the band **JANUARY 63** Charlie joins **FEBRUARY 63** Start of residency at the Station Hotel, Richmond **14th APRIL 63** The Beatles are in the audience at the Crawdaddy Club **JUNE 63** First single - 'Come On' - released **JULY 63** UK TV debut on 'Thank Your Lucky Stars' **SEPTEMBER 63** 1st UK tour, supporting the Everly Brothers and Bo Diddley **JANUARY 64** 2nd UK tour, first as headliners, with support including the Ronettes **FEBRUARY 64** 3rd UK tour, with John Leyton **APRIL 64** First album, 'The Rolling Stones', released **5th JUNE 64** First tour of the USA opens in San Bernadino, CA, two days after TV appearance on 'The Hollywood Palace Show', hosted by Dean Martin **24th JULY 64** Riot at the Empress Ballroom, Blackpool during summer tour of the UK **8th AUGUST 64** Riot at the Scheveningen opera house, The Hague **SEPTEMBER 64** 4th UK tour opens; support includes the Mojos and Inez and Charlie Foxx **OCTOBER 64** 2nd US tour, including debut on 'The Ed Sullivan Show' **JANUARY 65** 'The Rolling Stones No. 2' ➤

released. Debut Australia, NZ and Far East tour opens 18th MARCH 65 The infamous garage wall incident, during UK tour APRIL 65 Three nights at Olympia Theatre, Paris. 3rd US tour starts SEPTEMBER 65 'Out Of Our Heads' released. UK tour, with Spencer Davis Group, opens OCTOBER 65 4th US tour starts; support includes Patti LaBelle and the Blue Belles FEBRUARY 66 Australasian tour MARCH 66 European tour APRIL 66 'Aftermath' released JUNE 66 5th tour of USA with the McCoys and the Standells 23th SEPTEMBER 66 'Rolling Stones 66' tour of the UK opens at the Royal Albert Hall; support includes Ike and Tina Turner and the Yardbirds JANUARY 67 'Between The Buttons' released. Only appearance on 'Sunday Night At The London Palladium' TV show APRIL 67 Shows in Warsaw and Athens, during European tour JUNE 67 Mick and Keith encounter Her Majesty's Pleasure DECEMBER 67 'Their Satanic Majesties Request' released DECEMBER 68 'Beggars Banquet' released. The Rock And Roll Circus filmed JUNE 69 Brian leaves the Stones. Mick Taylor is announced as replacement 3rd JULY 69 Brian Jones dies 5th JULY 69 Stones play at free concert in Hyde Park NOVEMBER 69 6th US tour opens 6th DECEMBER 69 Free concert at Altamont Speedway, CA. 'Let It Bleed' released SEPTEMBER 70 Live album, 'Get Yer Ya-Ya's Out!', released. First European tour for 3 years DECEMBER 70 'Gimme Shelter', film on the 69 US tour, premieres in New York MARCH 71 UK tour, following decision to become tax exiles, includes Marquee Club date ➤

APRIL 71 'Sticky Fingers' released MAY 72 'Exile On Main Street' released. JUNE 72 American Tour 1972, with Stevie Wonder and Martha Reeves, filmed as the unreleased 'Cocksucker Blues' AUGUST 73 'Goats Head Soup' released SEPTEMBER 73 European tour opens OCTOBER 74 'It's Only Rock'n'Roll' released DECEMBER 74 Mick Taylor leaves APRIL 75 Ronnie Wood joins 1st MAY 75 1975 Tour Of The Americas, opening on 1st June, is announced; Stones play Fifth Avenue on the back of a flat-bed truck APRIL 76 'Black And Blue' released MAY 76 Six dates at Earl's Court during European tour AUGUST 76 Headline appearance at Knebworth Festival FEBRUARY 77 Keith's Canadian incident SEPTEMBER 77 'Love You Live', including set recorded at El Mocambo nightclub in Toronto, released JUNE 78 'Some Girls' released. 9th US tour opens 22nd APRIL 79 Gig at Oshawa Civic Auditorium, Ontario for Canadian National Institute for the Blind JUNE 80 'Emotional Rescue' released AUGUST 81 'Tattoo You' released SEPTEMBER 81 10th US tour opens MAY 82 European tour opens in Aberdeen NOVEMBER 83 'Undercover' released 12th DECEMBER 85 Ian Stewart dies FEBRUARY 86 Tribute gig to Ian Stewart at 100 Club, London MARCH 86 'Dirty Work' released JULY 89 Steel Wheels tour announced AUGUST 89 'Steel Wheels' released. Steel Wheels tour opens at Veterans Stadium, Philadelphia - includes first Tokyo dates ever MAY 90 Urban Jungle tour begins in Rotterdam APRIL 91 Live 'Flashpoint' album released JANUARY 93 Bill confirms he is leaving the Stones JULY 94 'Voodoo Lounge' released AUGUST 94 Voodoo Lounge tour opens at Robert F. Kennedy Memorial Stadium, Washington DC. The tour continues through 1996 NOVEMBER 94 Portion of gig in Dallas transmitted live on the Internet JANUARY 95 First ever Central and South American leg of a tour MARCH 95 During Voodoo Lounge tour, first Australian/NZ dates since 1973 SEPTEMBER 97 'Bridges To Babylon' released. Bridges To Babylon tour opens at Soldier Field, Chicago. The tour continues through 1999 ●

CAST OF CHARACTERS

Brief notes on the voices that can be heard in A Life On The Road

MICK JAGGER, KEITH RICHARDS, CHARLIE WATTS, RON WOOD and BILL WYMAN

need no introduction.

JIM CALLAGHAN left the army and landed his first job in band security with the Monkees in 1967. Two years later - at the Hyde Park concert - he asked Mick for a job with the Stones. His request was granted, but not until 1973, when he joined the band on their 1973 European tour after a stint working for various groups including Led Zeppelin. Since the 1975 Tour Of The Americas, he has been involved on every Stones tour and has worked on Mick and Keith's solo ventures (as well as with Bob Dylan). Jim was head of security on all the Steel Wheels/Urban Jungle, Voodoo Lounge and Bridges To Babylon tours.

BLONDIE CHAPLIN is a South African born multi-instrumentalist, singer and songwriter who first appeared with the Stones as a background vocalist and musician on both the Bridges To Babylon tour and album, after working on the Wingless Angels project with Keith. He is the lead vocalist and guitarist with Skollie, featuring his own songs, and has also performed and recorded with the Band, the Beach Boys, Bonnie Raitt, Phoebe Snow and Jennifer Warnes.

MICHAEL COHL first saw the Stones at Toronto's Maple Leaf Gardens in the 1960s. He has been a promoter since 1969, initially covering the whole of Canada (he was the Stones' Canadian promoter throughout the 70s) and then North America. After a period in the merchandising industry he was responsible for promoting the Steel Wheels/Urban Jungle tour of 1989/90, and has also been the Tour Director and Tour Promoter on Voodoo Lounge and Bridges To Babylon.

ALAN DUNN got involved with the Stones in 1967, initially as an driver/assistant to Mick. As the Stones tours began to grow in size so did his job, as he took on a variety of responsibilities alongside Ian Stewart, as road manager-cum-security-cum-wardrobe. He has been the band's Logistics Director since the 1972 American tour, overseeing all logistical aspects of the tours, from transportation to catering.

LISA FISCHER is, like Bernard Fowler. a graduate of the Steel Wheels/ Urban Jungle tour, which she joined after working for many years with Luther Vandross. She has also performed with Chaka Khan, Stevie Wonder, Mary J. Blige and Toni Braxton, as well as on Mick's solo work. Lisa won a Grammy for her vocal performance on the single 'How Can I Ease The Pain?' from the album So Intense, sings in the Disney animated film Hercules, and is a songwriter and arranger in her own right (she created the arrangements for Nuyorican Soul's 'Black Gold Of The Sun').

BERNARD FOWLER joined the Stones on backing vocals on the Steel Wheels tour, having worked with Herbie Hancock, Sly and Robbie and even Motorhead; the launch pad for his Stones career was singing on Mick Jagger's solo She's The Boss project in 1985. He has continued on both Voodoo Lounge and Bridges To Babylon and has contributed to solo projects for Keith Richards, Charlie Watts' jazz outings and Ronnie Wood. Bernard produced Ron's 1992 album Slide On This, and records and tours with his own group Nicklebag.

DARRYL JONES On the Voodoo Lounge album and subsequent tour, Darryl stepped - following extensive auditions - into the prestigious shoes of Bill Wyman as bass player with the Stones. He was already an experienced touring musician, having previously played alongside Miles Davis for four years, as well as Herbie Hancock. Darryl has also worked with Peter Gabriel, Sting, Madonna and Joe Cocker - and since the Voodoo Lounge tour has appeared as an actor in the movie Gridlock.

BOBBY KEYS After running into the Stones on their first US tour in 1964, while he was part of Bobby Vee's band, Bobby - born on the same day, month and year as Keith Richards - worked with Leon Russell, JJ Cale, and Delaney and Bonnie before delivering his first Stones sax solo on 'Live With Me' from the Let It Bleed album. As well as providing keynote solos on tracks like 'Brown Sugar', Bobby has toured with the band in 1971, 72 and 73, 81/82 and on the Steel Wheels/Urban Jungle, Voodoo Lounge and Bridges To Babylon tours, only missing the 1975 Tour of the Americas because he was on the road with Joe Cocker.

TONY KING was a promotion man at Decca Records when Chrissie Shrimpton, then Mick's girlfriend, took him to see the Stones at the Scene Club in Ham Yard. Tony subsequently went to work for the Stones just after they'd recorded 'Satisfaction', at Andrew Loog Oldham's request, and handled record promotion throughout 1965 and 1966. After a period working with the Beatles, Elton John and RCA in New York, he then re-turned to work with Mick in 1984 and with the Stones on the Steel Wheels tour, and has acted as press liaison for Mick on all the tours thereafter.

CHUCK LEAVELL Keyboardist with the Allman Brothers Band in the early 70s on albums like Laid Back and Brothers And Sisters, Chuck was a Muscle Shoals regular, working with artists including Dr. John and Hank Williams Jr, as well as the Allmans, and eventually forming his own outfit, Sea Level. He first toured with the Stones on the 1982 European tour (he was recommended to the band by Bill Graham), and has worked with them ever since, on both albums and tours, as well as for Eric Clapton, the Black Crowes, the Indigo Girls, Blues Traveller and George Harrison. He describes his role as 'keyboardist, archival arrangement and navigation expert'.

PRINCE RUPERT LOEWENSTEIN first met Mick in 1968, at which time he was a managing director of Leopold Joseph, the London merchant bankers. He was invited to take over the Stones' commercial matters in 1970, and was able to bring some sense of order to the Stones' then tangled and ineffective financial affairs. He has been their adviser ever since.

CAPTIONS & CREDITS

Credits are given spread by spread, with captions where information is available and relevant.

1

2   3

Top: Bridges to Babylon audience - LFI/Kevin Mazur.
Bottom: University of Illinois, Champaign IL, 15 November 1969 -
Rex Features/Ethan Russell

4   5

Voodoo Lounge - Musidor B.V./Claude Gassian

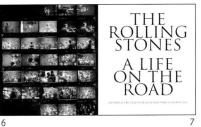

6   7

Contact sheet from North American tour October-December 1965-
Gered Mankowitz © Bowstir Ltd 1998

8   9

Musidor B.V./Anton Corbijn

10   11

Ron - from The Birds publicity shot. All other photos - Rex
Features/Dezo Hoffman

12   13

Brian - Rex Features/Dezo Hoffman. Right: on HMS Discovery,
London, August 1963 - Pictorial Press/Tony Gale. Keith's 3rd
quote, page 12 - Rolling Stone, August 1971

14   15

Musidor B.V./Eugene Adebari

16   17

Left: Marquee Club - LFI. Right: Musidor B.V./Claude Gassian

18   19

Left: El Mocambo Club, Toronto, March 1977 - Rex Features.
Right: The 100 Club, May 1982 - Munro Sounds archive/Michael Putland

20   21

Left: The Crawdaddy Club, May 1963 - Rex Features/Dezo Hoffman.
Right background: Marquee Club, 1963 - Pictorial Press

22   23

Left - Retna/King Collection. Right: poster for an August 1963 gig
in Liverpool that was cancelled because the venue had been
damaged by fire - Pictorial Press

24   25

Page 24 left - Musidor B.V./David Anderson. Page 24 right - Musidor B.V./Mikio Ariga. Page 25 top: on Ready Steady Go!, 1964 - Pictorial Press/Tony Gale. Page 25 bottom: on Ready Steady Go!, 1965 - Rex Features

26   27

Left - Munro Sounds archive. Right: on Ready Steady Go!, 1963 - Pictorial Press

28   29

From top: Musidor B.V./Eugene Adebari; Munro Sounds archive; Musidor B.V./Mikio Ariga

30   31

Page 30 top: Keith Richards at a campsite on an Apache reservation near Phoenix AZ, 6 December 1965 - Gered Mankowitz © Bowstir Ltd 1998. Page 30 bottom: Rex Features/Marc Sharratt. Page 31 left: Tour of the Americas, 1975 - Christopher Simon Sykes collection. Right: Voodoo Lounge - Musidor B.V./Mikio Ariga. Keith's 1st quote page 12 - Rolling Stone, August 1971

32   33

With Andrew Loog Oldham at RCA Studios, Hollywood CA, December 1965 - Gered Mankowitz © Bowstir Ltd 1998

34   35

Rex Features/Dezo Hoffman

36   37

Top left: press conference at Beverly Rodeo Hotel, Los Angeles, December 1965 - Gered Mankowitz © Bowstir Ltd 1998. Bottom left: at London Airport, 1964 - Rex Features. Right: North American tour October-December 1965 - Gered Mankowitz © Bowstir Ltd 1998. Keith's 1st quote, page 37 - Rolling Stone, August 1971. Mick's 2nd quote, page 37 - Rolling Stone, October 1968

38   39

Bill Graham Presents

40   41

Left: Playing cards with Nona Hendryx of Patti LaBelle and the Blue Belles on North American tour October-December 1965 - Gered Mankowitz © Bowstir Ltd 1998. Right: North American tour October-December 1965 - Gered Mankowitz © Bowstir Ltd 1998. Keith's quotes, page 40 - Rolling Stone, August 1971

42   43

Left: Voodoo Lounge - Musidor B.V./Claude Gassian. Right: October 1966 - Pictorial Press/Tony Gale. Background: New Elizabethan Ballroom, Belle Vue, Manchester, 9 August 1964 - Mirror Syndication International. Keith's quote, page 42 - Rolling Stone, August 1971

44   45

Page 44 top left - Rex Features. Page 44 top right: Bridges to Babylon press conference, Brooklyn Bridge, 18 August 1997 - Musidor B.V./Kevin Mazur. Page 44 bottom: Mick shopping at Cerutti's in Paris - Rex Features/Michel Ginies/SIPA Press. Page 45 top left: Niagara Falls, 1975 - Christopher Simon Sykes collection. Page 45 top right: Basel, 1990 - Musidor B.V./Claude Gassian. Page 45 centre - Retna/Rocky Winder. Page 45 bottom left: at London Airport en route to the USA, 23 June 1966 - Rex Features. Page 45 bottom right: Buenos Aires, February 1995 - Jane Rose

46   47

Page 46: Basel, Urban Jungle tour, 27 June 1990 - Musidor B.V./Claude Gassian. Page 47 top left - Rex Features. Page 47 bottom left: Festhalle, Frankfurt, 30 September 1973 - Retna/Michael Putland. Page 46 right: Earls Court, London, May 1976 - Retna/Michael Putland

"Get off my foreskin,

48   49

Louisiana State Fair, Shreveport LA, 20 November 1965 - Gered Mankowitz © Bowstir Ltd 1998

50   51

Keith and his Bentley - Gered Mankowitz © Bowstir Ltd 199

52   53

Page 52 main - Rex Features/Marc Sharratt. Page 52 inset - Retna/Richard E. Aaron. Pages 52-53 bottom: Voodoo Lounge - Musidor B.V./Claude Gassian. Page 53 top right - Rex Features

54   55

Page 54 top left: Voodoo Lounge, Japan, March 1995 - Musidor B.V./Mikio Ariga. Page 54 centre: 'Live at the Ten Spot', 1997 - Musidor B.V./Kevin Mazur. Page 54 bottom right: Brixton Academy, London, 19 July 1995 - All Action/Dave Hogan. Page 55 top: Bridges to Babylon - Musidor B.V./Albert Ferreira. Page 55 bottom - Musidor B.V./Albert Ferreira. Keith's quote, page 54 - Rolling Stone, August 1971

56   57

Left: leaving London Airport for the USA, 23 June 1966, via what the original press caption called "a hard struggle for the gather-no-moss boys" - Rex Features. Right - LFI

58   59

Left: Chuck Leavell, 1982 European tour - Musidor B.V./Denis O'Regan. Right: Jacksonville FL, August 1975 - Christopher Simon Sykes collection

60   61

Paris, 1990 - Musidor B.V./Claude Gassian

62   63

Page 62 top: 1976 - Pictorial Press. Page 62 bottom - Rex Features/SIPA/Thierry Bocon-Gibod. Page 63: 1982 European tour - Musidor B.V./Denis O'Regan

64   65

Left: Les Abattoirs, Paris, June 1976 - Rex Features/SIPA Press/Thierry Bocon-Gibod. Right: Voodoo Lounge - Musidor B.V./Mikio Ariga

66   67

Page 66 top left: 1992 European tour - Musidor B.V./Denis O'Regan. Page 66 top centre - Musidor B.V./Mikio Ariga. Page 66 top right - Rex Features/SIPA/Thierry Bocon-Gibod. Page 66 bottom right - Bill Graham Presents. Page 67 left - Rex Features. Page 67 right: Musidor B.V./Claude Gassian

68   69

Left: January 1967 - Rex Features/Bill Orchard. Right: Palazzo dello Sport, Rome, 6 April 1967 - Rex Features. Keith's quotes, page 68 - Rolling Stone, August 1971. Mick's 2nd quote, page 69 - Rolling Stone, October 1968

70   71

Page 70 top left - Munro Sounds archive. Page 70 bottom right - Retna/Michael Putland. Page 71 - Retna/Michael Putland

72 73

Left: Scotland, May 1982 - Retna/Michael Putland. Centre: returning from Berlin, the last show of the 1973 European tour - Retna/Michael Putland. Right - Rex Features/Marc Sharratt

74 75

'The Rolling Stones Rock And Roll Circus' images - Rex Features/David Polak/David Magnus; Munro Sounds archive/Michael Putland; Pictorial Press. Mick and Marianne Faithfull at the Duke of Bedford's party for the Supremes, King's Road, Chelsea, January 1968 - Pictorial Press. Beggars Banquet session June 1968 - Pictorial Press/Vinyl Experience. Keith's quote, page 74 - Rolling Stone, August 1971. Mick's 1st quote, page 74 - Rolling Stone, October 1968

76 77

Page 76: Mick and Darryl Jones - Musidor B.V./Claude Gassian. Page 77 top - LFI. Page 77 bottom: Brian pulling a 'nanker' face - Gered Mankowitz © Bowstir Ltd 1998

78 79

Left - Rex Features/Eugene Adebari. Right top and bottom- Musidor B.V./Claude Gassian

80 81

Page 80: on Ready Steady Go!, 1966 - Pictorial Press/Tony Gale. Page 81 left strip - Rex Features. Page 81 top right: on Ready Steady Go!, 1965 - Rex Features. Keith's quotes, page 81 - Rolling Stone, August 1971

82 83

Page 82: May 1968 - Pictorial Press. Page 83 top left - Munro Sounds archive/Eric Hayes. Page 83 centre left: at Supremes party, January 1968 - Pictorial Press. Page 83 bottom - Retna/King Collection. Page 83 right - Munro Sounds archive

84 85

Left - Rex Features. Right - Redferns/David Redfern. Mick's quotes, page 84 - Rolling Stone, July 1969

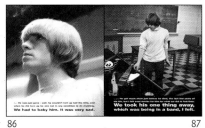

86 87

Both images: North American tour October-December 1965 - Gered Mankowitz © Bowstir Ltd 1998

88 89

Hyde Park, 5 July 1969 - LFI

90 91

Page 90: Hyde Park, 5 July 1969 - Retna/Michael Putland. Page 91 clockwise from top left: Mick and Marianne Faithfull - Retna/Michael Putland; Retna/Jak Kilby; Retna/Ray Stevenson; Mick Taylor introduced to the press, 13 June 1969 - Rex/Dezo Hoffman; Redferns/Peter Sanders; Retna/Ray Stevenson

92 93

Page 93 top left and right: Tour of the Americas 1975 - Christopher Simon Sykes collection. Page 93 bottom left and right: on the plane during the US tour November-December 1969 - Rex/Ethan Russell. Keith's 1st quote, page 92 - Rolling Stone, August 1971. Mick's 2nd quote, page 92 - Rolling Stone, December 1969

94 95

At Stephen Stills' house, Laurel Canyon CA, October-November 1969 - Rex Features/Ethan Russell

96 97

Free concert, Altamont Speedway, Livermore CA, 6 December 1969 - Jim Marshall

98 99

Page 98 - Munro Sounds archive. Page 99 top left: Jim Callaghan and Joe Seabrook - Musidor B.V./Paul Natkin. Page 99 top right - Munro Sounds archive. Page 99 background: Hyde Park, 5 July 1969 - Rex Features/Dezo Hoffman

100 101

Royal Albert Hall, 23 September 1966 - Pictorial Press

102 103

Page 102 top left - Michael Putland. All other images: Tour of Europe 1970 - Munro Sounds archive

104 105

Page 104: Munro Sounds archive. Page 105 top left - Munro Sounds archive. Page 105 bottom right: Hyde Park, 5 July 1969 - Redferns/Peter Sanders. Mick's quote, page 105 - Rolling Stone, July 1969

106 107

Rex Features/Dezo Hoffman

108 109

Left - Munro Sounds archive. Right: Mick Taylor wearing an afro wig, Deutschlandhalle, Berlin, 19 October 1973 - Retna/Michael Putland

110 111

Page 110 left strip from top: Bobby Keys and the New West Horns (Kent Smith, Andy Snitzer, Michael Davis), 1997 - Claude Gassian; the Uptown Horns (Arno Hecht, Crispin Cioe, Bob Funk, Hollywood Paul Litteral), 1990 - Musidor B.V./George Chin; Ian Stewart - Musidor B.V./Denis O'Regan; Bobby Keys and Jim Price, 1970 - Munro Sounds archive; Chuck Leavell - Musidor B.V./Claude Gassian; Matt Clifford - Musidor B.V./Eugene Adebari. Page 110 middle strip from top: Billy Preston, 1975 - Christopher Simon Sykes collection; Trevor Lawrence with Mick, 1973 - Retna/Michael Putland; Ollie Brown, 1975 - Christopher Simon Sykes collection. Page 111 left: Bernard Fowler - Musidor B.V./Mikio Ariga. Page 111 right: Darryl Jones - Musidor B.V./Kevin Mazur

112 113

Page 112: Lisa Fischer and Mick - Musidor B.V./Mikio Ariga. Page 113 top left: Bernard Fowler, Lisa and Blondie Chaplin, Bridges To Babylon - Musidor B.V./Albert Ferreira. Page 113 top right: Lisa and Leah Wood, Stade de France, Paris, 25 July 1998 - Claude Gassian. Page 113 bottom - Musidor B.V./Eugene Adebari

114 115

Page 114 top and bottom left: Marquee Club, 26 March 1971 - Pictorial Press. Page 114 bottom right - Rex Features. Page 115 left: France, 1971 - Munro Sounds archive. Page 115 right - Munro Sounds Archive

116 117

Clockwise from top left: Munro Sounds archive; Pictorial Press; Redferns/Fin Costello; Munro Sounds archive; Munro Sounds archive

118 119

Top left: Earls Court, London, May 1976 - Redferns/Dick Barnatt. Bottom left: L'Olympia, Paris, 20 October 1964 - Rex Features. Top right: Madison Square Garden - Redferns/Graham Wiltshire. Bottom right: Tour of the Americas 1975, Times Square, New York - Pictorial Press

120   121

Top left: 'Live at the Ten Spot', 1997 - Musidor B.V./Kevin Mazur. Bottom left - Musidor B.V./Claude Gassian. Top right: Tour of the Americas 1975 - Christopher Simon Sykes collection. Bottom right: Bridges to Babylon rig - both Diana Scrimgeour

122   123

Top left: lotus stage, Tour of the Americas 1975 - Pictorial Press/Waring Abbott. Bottom left: 1981/82 tour - Mark Fisher. Top right: Steel Wheels - Mark Fisher. Bottom right: Voodoo Lounge - Mark Fisher

124   125

All images: Bridges to Babylon - Mark Fisher

126   127

Page 126: Musidor B.V./Claude Gassian. Page 127 from top: Tour of the Americas 1975 - Christopher Simon Sykes collection; Musidor B.V./Claude Gassian; Darryl Jones - Musidor B.V./Claude Gassian

128   129

1973 - Redferns/Ian Dickson

130   131

Page 130 - Musidor B.V./Denis O'Regan. Page 131 clockwise from top left: Musidor B.V./Denis O'Regan; Munro Sounds archive; 1982 tour cake - Musidor B.V./Denis O'Regan; shepherd's pie cake - Jane Rose; shepherd's pie, Stade de France, Paris, 25 July 1998 - Dan Einzig; Seattle, July 1975 - Christopher Simon Sykes collection

132   133

Main shot: Stade de France, Paris, 25 July 1998 - Claude Gassian. Top row from left: Chuch Magee - Marjo Nieminen/Claude Gassian; Jake Berry - Claude Gassian; Chuch Magee, Steve Shepherd and Pierre de Beauport - Chris Wade-Evans; Pierre de Beauport - Claude Gassian; Claude Gassian

134   135

All photos: Stade de France, Paris, 25 July 1998 - Claude Gassian

136   137

Page 136 from left - Musidor B.V./Denis O'Regan; January 1982 - Munro Sounds archive/Sara Marks; Musidor B.V./George Chin. Page 137: Musidor B.V./Dennis O'Regan

138   139

Page 138 top - Musidor B.V./Mikio Ariga. Page 138 bottom - Musidor B.V./Paul Natkin. Page 139: with the England Football Team, 1974 - Retna/Michael Putland

140   141

Page 140 top left: backstage, State Theatre, Kilburn, London, 22 December 1974 - Redferns/Mick Gold. Page 140 bottom right: Madrid, June 1990 - Musidor B.V./Claude Gassian. Page 141 - Munro Sounds Archive

142   143

Retna/Michael Putland

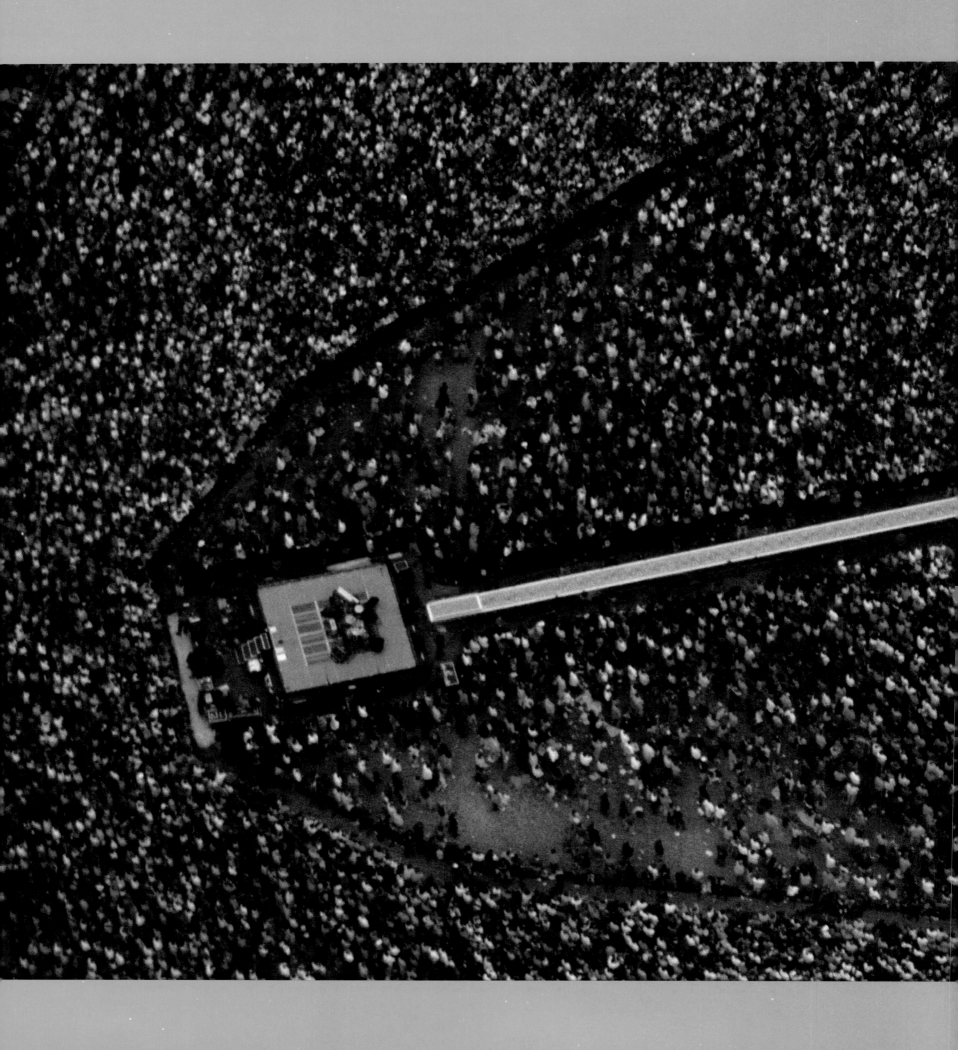

144   145

1978 - Rex Features

146   147

Page 146 top left and top right: 1964 - Rex Features. Page 146 bottom - Munro Sounds archive. Page 147 top row left to right - Munro Sounds archive/Michael Putland; Munro Sounds archive/Michael Putland; Rex Features. Page 147 middle row from left - Munro Sounds archive/Michael Putland; Retna/Michael Putland; Musidor B.V./George Chin. Page 147 bottom row from left - Rex Features; Musidor B.V./Mikio Ariga; Munro Sounds archive/Michael Putland; Musidor B.V./Claude Gassian

148   149

Page 148 top row left to right - Musidor B.V./Denis O'Regan; Musidor B.V./Paul Natkin; Musidor B.V./Denis O'Regan; Musidor B.V./Denis O'Regan. Page 148 middle row from left - Musidor B.V./George Chin; Christopher Simon Sykes collection; Musidor B.V./Denis O'Regan. Page 148 bottom row from left - Musidor B.V./Denis O'Regan; Musidor B.V./Mikio Ariga; Musidor B.V./Eugene Adebari; Pictorial Press. Page 149: Musidor B.V./Claude Gassian

150   151

Page 150: 1964 - Rex Features/Michael Ward. Page 151 main: Ron and Caroline Clements - Musidor B.V./Claude Gassian. Page 151 inset: Delilah Rose - photograph by Jane Rose (Keith's manager)

152   153

All photos: Tour of the Americas 1975 - Christopher Simon Sykes collection

154   155

Left: New York, Tour of the Americas 1975 - Christopher Simon Sykes collection; right - Christopher Simon Sykes collection

156   157

Page 156 from top: Christopher Simon Sykes collection; Christopher Simon Sykes collection; Retna/Michael Putland; Christopher Simon Sykes collection. Page 157: the flat-bed truck, Fifth Avenue, New York, 1 May 1975 - Pictorial Press

158   159

Tour of the Americas 1975 - all images from Christopher Simon Sykes collection

160   161

Left - Musidor B.V/Mikio Ariga. Right - Musidor B.V./George Chin

162   163

Bridges To Babylon - Musidor B.V.

164   165

Page 164 - Munro Sounds archive. Page 165 top - Musidor B.V./Claude Gassian. Page 165 bottom: Dodger Stadium, Los Angeles, 10 November 1997 - Musidor B.V./Kevin Mazur

166   167

Left - Retna/Janet Macoska. Right - Musidor B.V./David Anderson

168 169
Left - LFI. Right: Bristol, 9 March 1971 - Redferns/David Redfern

170 171
1982 - Rex Features/Andrew Spearman

172 173
Page 172 - Michael Putland. Page 173 all images - Munro Sounds Archive

174 175
Page 174 top left: Montauk, Long Island NY, May 1975 - Christopher Simon Sykes collection. Page 174 bottom right - Michael Putland. Page 175 - Musidor B.V./Claude Gassian

176 177
1979 - Retna/Neal Preston

178 179
Page 178 top left: Prince Rupert Loewenstein, 1975 - Christopher Simon Sykes collection. Page 178 centre: Knebworth Festival, 21 August 1976 - Retna/Michael Putland. Page 178 bottom left: Palladium, New York, 19 June 1978 - Retna/Michael Putland. Page 179: 1976 - Retna/Michael Putland

180 181
Left - Musidor B.V./Claude Gassian. Right - Musidor B.V./Mikio Ariga

182 183
1964 - Rex Features

184 185
Left: Musidor B.V./Claude Gassian. Right: Tour of the Americas 1975 - Christopher Simon Sykes collection. Keith's 1st quote, page 184 - Rolling Stone, August 1971

186 187
Bridges To Babylon: Musidor B.V./Denis O'Regan

188 189
Page 188 clockwise from top left: Mick, Keith and Marlon Richards, 1973 - Retna/Michael Putland; Marlon and Angela Richards, 1979 - Rex/Richard Young; Keith, Anita Pallenberg and Marlon, Helsinki, 1970 - Rex Features; Ron, Bianca Jagger and Mick, 1979 - Rex Features; Shirley and Serafina Watts - Munro Sounds archive.
Page 189 top row from left: Keith, Patti, Alexandra and Theodora Richards - Jane Rose; Mick and Jerry - Musidor B.V./Claude Gassian; Jo (top) and Tyrone (right) Wood - Musidor B.V/Denis O'Regan. Page 189 middle row from left: Bill and Stephen Wyman, 1965 - Rex Features; Ron, Keith and families, 16 July 1993 - All Action; Mick, Jerry, James and Elizabeth Jagger, 1987 - Rex Features. Page 189 bottom: Charlie and Serafina Watts - Rex Features

190 191
Musidor B.V./Claude Gassian

192   193
Left - LFI/Nick Towers. Right - Munro Sounds Archive

194   195
Ashton Gate Park, Bristol, 27 June 1982 - Redferns/Graham Wiltshire

196   197
1981/82 tour, page 196 top row from left: Paris, June 1982 - Rex Features; Musidor
B.V/Denis O'Regan; Retna/Michael Putland. Page 196 middle row from left - Rex
Features/Philippe Hamon; Musidor B.V/Denis O'Regan; Musidor B.V./Denis O'Regan.
Page 196 bottom row from left: (inset) Ian Stewart - Musidor B.V./Denis O'Regan;
(below inset) Roundhay Park, Leeds, 25 July 1982 - Pictorial Press; Musidor B.V./Denis
O'Regan; Meadowlands, East Rutherford NJ, November 1981 - Retna/Andy Freeberg.
Page 197 top row from left - Musidor B.V/Denis O'Regan; Rex Features/Andrew
Spearman; Retna/Michael Putland. Page 197 middle row from left - Musidor B.V/Denis
O'Regan; poster - Bill Graham Presents; Musidor B.V/Denis O'Regan. Page 197 bottom
row from left - Musidor B.V/Denis O'Regan; Rex Features; Retna/Michael Putland

198   199
All images - Musidor B.V/Denis O'Regan

200   201
Clockwise from far left - Retna/Michael Putland; Rex
Features; Retna/Michael Putland; Retna/Michael Putland;
Retna/Michael Putland; Retna/Michael Putland

202   203
Page 202 top: Arnold Dunn leads the band out, Stade de France, Paris, 25 July
1998 - Claude Gassian. Page 202 bottom: Arnold Dunn also leads the band out
- Musidor B.V/Claude Gassian. Page 203: 1976 - Pictorial Press

204   205
Left - Retna/Holland. Right: Apollo Theatre, Glasgow, May 1976 -
Retna/Michael Putland

206   207
Page 206 top - Munro Sounds archive. Page 206 bottom - Rex Features.
Page 207 clockwise from top left: Musidor B.V/Claude Gassian; Munro
Sounds archive; Musidor B.V/George Chin; Munro Sounds archive;
Get Yer Ya-Ya's Out! session - Munro Sounds archive; Rex Features

208   209
Left - Munro Sounds Archive. Right: Charlie and Shirley Watts,
Paris, 1990 - Musidor B.V/Claude Gassian

210   211
1973 - Retna/Michael Putland

212   213
Keith's hand - Musidor B.V./Mikio Ariga. Mick's mouth - Pictorial Press.
Charlie's foot - Musidor B.V./Eugene Adebari. Charlie's hand - Musidor
B.V./Claude Gassian. Keith's foot - Musidor B.V./Claude Gassian

214   215
Keith solo, April 1988 - Musidor B.V. Mick solo - Musidor B.V.
Charlie's big band - Munro Sounds archive/Ken Regan

216   217
Left: Munro Sounds archive. Right: Munro Sounds archive

218   219
Page 218 from top - Redferns/Richie Aaron; Munro Sounds archive; Bobby with Gene Barge, 1982 - Musidor B.V./Denis O'Regan. Page 219 main - Munro Sounds archive. Page 219 inset: Bridges To Babylon - Musidor B.V./Mikio Ariga

220   221
Left: the Bridges To Babylon golf team from left: Dennis 'The Griff' Griffin, Kent Smith, Bobby Keys, Michael Davis, Mike 'Coach' Sexton, Jake Cohl and Michael Cohl (founding member!) - photo by Michael Davis. Right - LFI

222   223
Left - Rex Features/Bob Grant. Right: US tour 1981 - Retna/Michael Putland

224   225
Page 224 top - Musidor B.V./Eugene Adebari. Page 224 bottom - Musidor B.V./Claude Gassian. Page 225: Musidor B.V./Kevin Mazur. Mick's quote - Rolling Stone, December 1995

226   227
All Steel Wheels/Urban Jungle images - Musidor B.V./Paul Natkin/Claude Gassian/Eugene Adebari/George Chin/Robert Duyos. Posters - Chris Eborn collection

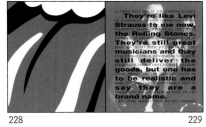

228   229
Right: Empire Pool, Wembley, 1973 - Retna/Michael Putland

230   231
Musidor B.V./Claude Gassian

232   233
Page 232 - Retna/Michael Putland. Page 233 main - Musidor B.V./Claude Gassian. Page 233 inset - Musidor B.V./Claude Gassian

234   235
Page 234 left strip from top - Rex Features; Rex Features; Munro Sounds archive; Munro Sounds archive. Page 234 right strip from top - Munro Sounds archive; Munro Sounds archive; Munro Sounds archive/Michael Putland; Munro Sounds archive. Page 235 - Redferns/Val Wilmer

236   237
Page 236 - LFI. Page 237 top: Mick with Ahmet Ertegun of Atlantic Records and Peter Rudge, Earls Court, May 76 - Retna/Michael Putland. Page 237 bottom - Retna/Michael Putland

238   239
Axl Rose and Mick, Convention Center, Atlantic City NJ, December 1989 - Musidor B.V./Kevin Mazur

240   241   242   243   244   245

Background: Munro Sounds/George Chin. Backstage visitors: George Harrison - Christopher Simon Sykes collection. Bianca Jagger and Andy Warhol, New York, 1975 - Christopher Simon Sykes collection. Bonnie Raitt, August 1994 - Jane Rose. Sheryl Crow, Hard Rock's The Joint, Las Vegas, 15 February 1998 - Musidor B.V./Kevin Mazur. Honor Blackman, May 1965 - Pictorial Press/Tony Gale. Linda and Paul McCartney, Palladium, New York, 19 June 1978 - Retna/Michael Putland. Brad Pitt, Hard Rock's The Joint, Las Vegas, 15 February 1998 - Musidor B.V./Kevin Mazur. Elton John, 1975 - Danny Lee/Christopher Simon Sykes collection. Howlin' Wolf, 1975 - Christopher Simon Sykes collection. HRH Princess Margaret and Ned Ryan, Earls Court, May 1976 - Retna/Michael Putland. Prince Rupert Loewenstein and Michael Cohl, August 1994 - Jane Rose. Peter Tosh and Bob Marley - Palladium, New York, 19 June 1978 - Retna/Michael Putland. Bob Dylan on stage - Retna/Gary Gershoff. Lenny Kravitz - Jane Rose. Nicole Kidman and Tom Cruise, Bruce Springsteen and Patti Scialfa - Musidor B.V./Albert Ferreira

Left - Musidor B.V./Paul Natkin; centre - Diana Scrimgeour; right - Musidor B.V./Eugene Adebar

Top left - Musidor B.V./Albert Ferreira. Bottom left - Musidor B.V./Albert Ferreira. Top right - Musidor B.V./Mikio Ariga. Bottom right - Musidor B.V./Albert Ferreira

246   247   248   249   250   251

Musidor B.V./David Anderson

Left both: Musidor B.V./Claude Gassian. Right: after the finale, Olympiahalle, Munich, September 1973 - Retna/Michael Putland

Musidor B.V./Claude Gassian

252   253   254   255   256   257

Page 252 main - Diana Scrimgeour. Page 252 inset: Moscow, 11 August 1998 - Tony King/Dora Loewenstein. Page 253 top left - Musidor B.V./Paul Natkin; top right - Diana Scrimgeour; bottom left - Musidor B.V./Paul Natkin; bottom right - Musidor B.V./Paul Natkin

Bridges To Babylon, Dodger Stadium, Los Angeles, 10 November 1997 - Musidor B.V./Kevin Mazur

Musidor B.V

258   259   260   261   262   263

Bridges To Babylon - Musidor B.V./Albert Ferreira

264   265

Left - Musidor B.V./Kevin Mazur. Right: Madison Square Garden, New York,
16 January 1998 - Musidor B.V./Kevin Mazur

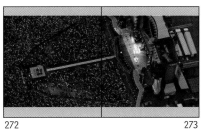

272   273

Bridges To Babylon - Musidor B.V./Thomas Rosenthal

280   281

Keith and Suzi Stokes - Musidor B.V./Claude Gassian

282   283

Backstage, Paris, Stade de France, 25 July 1998 - Claude Gassian

284   285

Background: Musidor B.V./Claude Gassian

286   287

Musidor B.V./Paul Natkin

288

Front endpaper
Gered Mankowitz © Bowstir Ltd 1998

Back endpaper
Musidor B.V./Claude Gassian

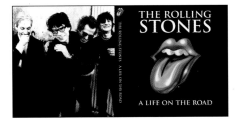

KEITH: We're still learning and we'll never stop.

You never know it all.

THE ROLLING STONES
A LIFE ON THE ROAD

INTERVIEWS by JOOLS HOLLAND and DORA LOEWENSTEIN

CONCEIVED AND COMPILED by DORA LOEWENSTEIN
with PHILIP DODD

Art direction and design by David Costa and Dan Einzig of Wherefore Art?,
assisted by Rachel Godfrey, Emma Smillie, Fiona Andreanelli and Janfranco Caro,
acknowledging the invaluable input of Nicky Hames and Philip Dodd

Additional interview material from Straight Arrow Publishers Company, L.P., 1968, 1969,
1971, 1995, all rights reserved, reprinted by permission; and from '25 x 5', produced and directed by
Andrew Salt © Promotour US.

Dora Loewenstein: I have to thank many people who have helped me make this book possible. I am sure that in this process I will omit a few crucial names and for that I would like to apologise in advance.

Obviously, my first thanks go to the Rolling Stones, without whom this book would not exist. My next thanks go to my father, Prince Rupert Loewenstein, who has played a crucial role in every step of the way. Jools Holland gets my heartfelt thanks, not only for his hard work but also his immense stamina 'on the road', where he kept a 24-hour waking day to attain the interview material for this book.

I would have liked to distinguish the different ways in which people have helped with this project, but alas there is no time or space. I hope that this alphabetical list will serve the purpose and offend no one.

So, my thanks to: Bob Bender, Jo Bergman, Bill Graham Presents, Susie Boone, Rowan Brade, Alvinia Bridges, Jim Callaghan, Cheryl Ceretti, Blondie Chaplin, Caroline Clements, Coach, Michael Cohl, David Costa, Fran Curtis, Sherry Daly, Mike Davis, Pierre de Beauport, Manfredi della Gherardesca, Philip Dodd, Bernard Doherty, Alan Dunn, Arnold Dunn, Chris Eborn, Torje Eike, Dan Einzig, Ahmet Ertegun, Lisa Fischer, Mark Fisher, Bernard Fowler, Anouk Fundarek, Lil Gary, Christobel Holland, Jerry Jagger, Darryl Jones, Sjaak Joritsmaa, Mark Kaylor, Paige Kevan, Bobs Keys, Tony King, Shelley Lazar, Chuck Leavell, Richard Leher, Paul Loasby, Princess Josephine Loewenstein, Camilla McGrath, Val McCartney, Chuch Magee, Bessie Mageri, Barry 'Spin' Mindel, Rebecca Nichols, Sophie Norman, Rob O'Connor, Eck Ogilvie-Grant, Miranda Payne, Mal Peachey, Jerry Pompili, Joe Rascoff, Patti Richards, Jaye Riggio, Jane Rose, Tony Russell, Roz Scott, Joe Seabrook, Steve Shepherd, Rob Shreeve, Kent Smith, Andy Snitzer, Lynne Tanzmann, Emma Tiffin, Clare Turner, Arabella Unwin, Fay van Engelen, Ed Victor, Chris Wade-Evans, Debbie Walker, Shirley Watts, Ethan Weber, Alan Williams, Josephine Wood, Patrick Woodroffe, Isabelle Work.

Jools Holland: I would like to thank Dora and Rupert Loewenstein, Tony King, Philip Dodd, all the musicians and crew, and - most of all - the band. I spent many hours in their homes, hotel suites and motor vehicles. I am most grateful for their hospitality and I would like to apologise for any stains, spillages, tears and laughter that may have got left in their quarters. On behalf of myself and my Rhythm and Blues Orchestra I take this opportunity to salute The Kings.

The publishers would also like to thank Bethany Smith at Raindrop Services; Steve Daly and Heather Nedwell at Munro Sounds; Emily Hedges and Juliette Brightmore for picture research, and all the photographers and picture agencies for their patience; Di Skinner for transcribing the tapes; Zoe Lyall for editorial assistance; Ian Welch at Northdown Publishing for research assistance; Danny Reynolds, Vince Nichols and the team at Media Repro.

PENGUIN STUDIO
Published by the Penguin Group
Penguin Putnam Inc., 375 Hudson Street,
New York, New York 10014, U.S.A.
Penguin Books Ltd, 27 Wrights Lane,
London W8 5TZ, England
Penguin Books Australia Ltd, Ringwood,
Victoria, Australia
Penguin Books Canada Ltd, 10 Alcorn Avenue,
Toronto, Ontario, Canada M4V 3B2
Penguin Books (N.Z.) Ltd, 182-190 Wairau Road,
Auckland 10, New Zealand
Penguin India, 210 Chiranjiv Tower, 43 Nehru Place,
New Delhi 11009, India

Penguin Books Ltd, Registered Offices:
Harmondsworth, Middlesex, England

First published in 1998 by Penguin Studio,
a member of Penguin Putnam Inc.

1 3 5 7 9 10 8 6 4 2

Copyright © Promopub B.V. 1998
All rights reserved

ISBN 0-670-88051-5

CIP data available
Printed in Great Britain

AFTERWORD

BY PRINCE RUPERT LOEWENSTEIN

HERE ARE A FEW REFLECTIONS ON NEARLY 30 YEARS OF ROLLING STONES PERFORMANCES, MY FIRST EXPERIENCE OF WHICH WAS THE OPEN AIR CONCERT IN HYDE PARK IN JULY OF 1969; MICK BEGAN IT BY READING EXTRACTS FROM SHELLEY'S ADONAIS, AS A MEMORIAL FOR BRIAN JONES. THIS WAS TO AN AUDIENCE OF, IT IS SAID, SOME 250,000 PEOPLE TO BE KEPT IN ORDER BY THE HELL'S ANGELS, HAD THIS BEEN NEEDED. 29 YEARS LATER, ON THE EVE OF MICK'S 55TH BIRTHDAY, THE STONES PLAYED TO 80,000 FANS IN THE STADE DE FRANCE FOR ITS OPENING ROCK SHOW.

Looking round the Stade, where a few weeks before the World Cup Final had taken place, the thought occurred to me that in performances stretching from Hyde Park and Shelley to this huge international audience in Paris, one unifying theme was the Englishness of the band, which at the same time has a universal appeal and uses the support both of artists and professionals from a wide range of countries. Mick and Keith, Charlie and Ronnie (and Bill in his day), could not be anything but English and each is a proud and worthy representative of his country in an international context. Could this be an example for a 'Europe des Patries'?

What is the secret of this amazing success over such a long period? Of course many ingredients go into the pot: first and foremost the quality of the music which has an enduring attraction, then the engaging visual effects and the sheer energy projected by the band. But this is not all, especially in a stadium (let alone a field) where the size of the place dwarfs the performance and distances the sound. This is notwithstanding the fact that in the last few years there have been great advances on a technical level such as the huge video screens and good amplification. In earlier days - perhaps it was Turtle Beach in 1975? - I remember a stadium to whose distant top I clambered. The fans were packed in and enjoying themselves hugely. I asked

them the reason, since they could neither see the band nor hear the sound. "It's the Stones, man!" they replied. "They are **great**."

Then, too, there is now a feeling of nostalgia. The bulk of American and European audiences today have been fans for many years and they relive their past excitement. However, when the band plays in places where they have not been before, such as the Argentine, it is the teenage audience, as it was in Europe 30 years ago, which is the keenest.

Perhaps like all good secrets it cannot be revealed, but part of the answer is the indefinable attraction of star quality: the glamour, or capacity to mystify and dazzle, that a person can project to a vast crowd. Great orators and statesmen, Churchill on the wireless during the war, Hitler at Nuremburg (helped as he was by his lighting man and choreographer, Speer, on the very field the Stones played on the Bridges To Babylon tour) have this, as do the very few actors and singers who are the stars that we have among us today. It is in this minute company that Mick is numbered; but alone would the effect be so potent or indeed sufficient? What is unique is that this is but a part of the Stones' magic: each of Keith, Charlie and Ronnie add their own enormous talent and professionalism to the mix to make what is still the greatest rock show on earth.

"goodnight and thank you"

"The Stones have now left the building"